BEHIND THE PLATE

BEHIND THE PLATE

A Catcher's View of the Braves Dynasty

Javy Lopez with Gary Caruso

TRIUMPH
BOOKS

Library of Congress Cataloging-in-Publication Data

Lopez, Javy, 1970–
  Behind the plate : a catcher's view of the Braves dynasty / Javy Lopez
with Gary Caruso.
    p. cm.
  ISBN 978-1-60078-653-2 (hardback)
  1. Lopez, Javy, 1970– 2. Baseball players—Puerto Rico—Biography. 3. Atlanta Braves
(Baseball team) I. Caruso, Gary. II. Title.
  GV865.L68A3 2012
  796.357092—dc23
  [B]
                                    2011043671

This book is available in quantity at special discounts for your group or organization. For further information, contact:

Triumph Books LLC
542 South Dearborn Street
Suite 750
Chicago, Illinois 60605
(312) 939–3330
Fax (312) 663–3557
www.triumphbooks.com

Printed in U.S.A.
ISBN: 978-1-60078-653-2
Design by Patricia Frey
Photos courtesy of the author unless otherwise indicated

*In loving memory of
my sweet ma, Evelia Torres*

———————————————

CONTENTS

BEHIND
THE PLATE

IN THE BOOK!

ANYONE WHO PLAYS PROFESSIONAL BASEBALL PLAYS FOR THE love of the game, as well as for the money and the perks that go along with it. If you have that kind of talent—enough talent to be paid to play baseball—you probably love to play the game. Some players like it more than others do, and maybe a few don't truly love it at all. But that's rare.

I mean, what's not to like? Sure, there are parts of it that aren't fun—traveling in the middle of the night and being away from home a lot, for example. When you do it every day for six or seven months, it's not as glamorous as most people think it is. But you're playing baseball for a living—a very, very good living. It's a dream come true!

In my case, and I think in most players' cases, you don't just play baseball to play it. Regardless of what kind of player you are, I think you want to reach certain goals and maybe eventually set records. And with all the records they keep in baseball, it's possible for most players—if they're good enough, or if they're in the right place at the right time—to someday get their name in the record book.

You don't necessarily have to be a Hall of Famer to be in the record book. You don't have to be Hank Aaron. There's room for a lot of names in there, and I think every player would like to have his name in the book, whether it's for a few weeks, a few seasons, or many years.

I know I wanted to have my name in there. I wanted to leave my mark when I retired.

One of my first goals after I reached the majors full-time in 1994 was to make the National League All-Star team, and I did that three times (1997, 1998, and 2003).

I also wanted to win a Silver Slugger Award, which recognizes the best hitter in the league at each position. The managers and coaches vote on it every year, and I won that in 2003.

Then I wanted to win a Gold Glove. It's sort of like the Silver Slugger, but it's for fielding rather than hitting. By 2003 I was 32 years old and already had nine full seasons in the big leagues and late-season call-ups in two others. But I was getting older, and I knew that my chances of winning a Gold Glove were dwindling, even though I was working harder and harder on my catching.

I was pretty close to winning a Gold Glove at one point. As a matter of fact, I thought I should have won it in 1998 over Charles Johnson, in my opinion. Johnson, who was traded from the Marlins to the Dodgers on May 14 that year, had eight errors, a .992 fielding percentage, and threw out 40 percent of attempted base stealers. I had just five errors, a .995 fielding percentage, and threw out 34 percent of base stealers. But I never achieved my goal of winning a Gold Glove. I know I wasn't the best catcher in the world, but I know I had years when I could have won it. That's a very valuable award for a catcher, and I really wanted to win it.

After the 2002 season, things weren't looking too good for me in terms of setting any kind of significant records. In fact, that was the furthest thing from my mind. I just wanted to get my career back on track, because I had posted career lows—or close to it—in most hitting stats: a .233 batting average, 11 home runs, and 52 runs batted in. It was an awfully disappointing season from a personal standpoint. Rather than complain and cry about it, though, I decided to take care of it. Right after the season, I started working out. I said, "Let's fix it!"

The first thing I did was start losing weight. I began working out like I'd never worked out in my life, and that's a lot, because I always worked out. That off-season, though, I was working out twice a day.

At the time, I was having problems with my marriage, which I'll discuss later. Working out was the one thing that helped me forget about all that. I was a workaholic and lost 25 pounds, down to 220 from 245.

Even though I felt great, my marriage was still in the back of my mind. I didn't have the best spring training, but I felt great physically. I was hustling and running pretty well.

Just like any other season, I started kind of slowly. But this year was different. I needed to get my bat going, and for a very good reason. I was going home to Puerto Rico to play for the first time.

THAT WAS THE YEAR THAT MAJOR LEAGUE BASEBALL DECIDED that the Montreal Expos would play 22 games in Puerto Rico. Attendance in Montreal wasn't good, and MLB was considering moving the team or possibly even eliminating it, along with another franchise. So the Expos played games in San Juan, Puerto Rico, at Hiram Bithorn Stadium in 2003 and 2004 before relocating to Washington, D.C., in 2005 and becoming the Nationals.

The Braves were one of the first teams scheduled to travel to Puerto Rico. We were going there the third week of the season, April 15 through 17. I was excited about it, but I was worried also. We played our first seven games—and I still didn't have a home run. The last thing I wanted was to go to Puerto Rico with a zero in my home run column.

Just before we left for Puerto Rico, we played a three-game series against the Marlins in Miami. I went 1-for-4 in the first game. Just a single. Still no home runs.

The next night (April 12), I batted against Carl Pavano in the fourth inning. He had already struck me out in the second inning and had me this time with two outs and no one on base. He threw me a fastball inside, and all I did was use my hands. I didn't use my body at all, but I got a hold of it, and the ball barely cleared the fence.

I thought, *Yes! At least I'm going to Puerto Rico with* HR 1 *next to my name!*

Sometimes it seems the toughest hit to get is the first one of the season. Same thing with home runs. It sure was the case for me in 2003.

I didn't play the last game in Florida on Sunday, and then we had an off day on Monday. By then I was really looking forward to going home. It was the first time I played for the Braves back home, and it was a really big deal. My youngest sister, Elaine, had a party for us in San Juan. It was at a club on a pier where the big cruise ships come in. There was food, drinks, a band, a lot of guests, and the whole Braves team. Even my dad was there. The place was packed! Everybody had a tremendous time.

We stayed at the El Conquistador Resort, which is owned by the Waldorf Astoria and is one of the top luxury hotels in Puerto Rico. It's located right on the east coast, and they also own a little island nearby named Palomino Island. My brother-in-law's family owns 10 percent of that island, and they have a house there with guest quarters, kayaks, jet skis—everything. The hotel rented the rest of the island to my brother-in-law's family for that day. The hotel has a cable car that takes guests down to the ferry, and then the ferry takes people to the island.

The day after the party, everyone met—well, those who were able to wake up early! There were about 10 of us. We took a bus down to the wharf, where my sister had a boat waiting to take us to the island.

Remember, it was a day off for the team. And it's a good thing it was!

We spent the entire day on the island, eating and relaxing on the water. Andruw Jones, Rafael Furcal, Marcus Giles, Vinny Castilla, Jung Bong, Robert Fick, Henry Blanco, and Ray King were all there, among others.

We had an unbelievable time. The thing I remember most is Vinny Castilla and Rafael Furcal getting a ticket from the police for running too fast, too close on the jet skis. We all got a big laugh out of that.

When we finally got back to the hotel, we all crashed. But we were ready to go the next day.

There were big crowds for the games, and a lot of fans had signs supporting me. That stadium holds about 18,000 fans, and it was pretty full for all three games. I'm sure there were more people than there would have been had we played in Montreal. It certainly was a better baseball atmosphere because there weren't many empty seats like there often were in Montreal's Olympic Stadium.

There are a lot of Braves fans in Puerto Rico because our games were broadcast on TBS for many years, and they finally got a chance to see us play in person. I wanted to look good, but I ended the first day 0-for-4. Ground-outs my first two times up, then a fly to center and a strikeout. The next game was more of the same—another 0-for-4. At least I didn't strike out that game—two ground balls and two fly-outs.

Back-to-back collars. Great! Maybe I was trying too hard.

My dad was a nervous wreck. They were showing him and my sister in the stands on TV all the time. Every time I came to the plate, the cameras were all over them.

Fortunately, even though I didn't hit, I looked good behind the plate, and we won. The Expos were playing well; before we got there, they'd just swept their first four games in Puerto Rico from the Mets.

But we came down and did the opposite—we swept them. The first two games were close. We won the first one 2–1 in 10 innings and then won the second one 3–2. Actually, the third game was close too, though you wouldn't know it from the final score. And I finally had a lot to do with that.

I remember asking Jung Bong, the pitcher from South Korea, if I could use his bat that game—just to do something different. He said, "Sure."

I got a base hit in the second inning and scored to tie the game 2–2. Joking around, I asked for the ball, like it was my first hit in the big leagues. It was my first big-league hit in Puerto Rico, after all.

I grounded out in my second at-bat in the third inning and flied out in the fifth. But in my fourth at-bat, I hit a home run with a man on in the seventh inning to break a 6–6 tie and give us an 8–6 lead.

The whole stadium was going nuts. My dad was jumping up and down, celebrating. I never thought it was going to happen, and it sure felt great.

Unfortunately, the Expos came back to score two runs in the eighth to tie the game. In the ninth, I came up with two runners on and struck out. I could have won the game right there, but we wound up going extra innings for the second time in three games. In the end, I was glad we did.

We got two runs in the top of the 10th to take the lead, and then I came up with the bases loaded. I hit a grand slam off Rocky Biddle to wrap up a six-run inning and a 14–8 win. I was 3-for-6 for the day with two home runs and six RBIs. It was nice to get back on track after those first two games.

I'm just glad it happened. It was nuts after the game—everybody was very happy, especially my dad and my sister.

Everyone wanted autographs, and the media wanted interviews. There wasn't much time to celebrate, though, because we had to get on a plane to come back home. We had a game the next night in Atlanta against the Phillies.

I was only hitting .234 going into that last game in Puerto Rico, but those three hits raised my average to .264, and I finished the year at .328—a career high. I sure didn't know it at the time, but from that point on, 2003 was a year to remember—a career year.

I LOOK BACK ON THAT LAST GAME IN PUERTO RICO as really the start of my best season in the big leagues. After that series, I started consistently hitting home runs. I don't know if I caught fire because we had been in Puerto Rico or if it would have happened anyway.

I do remember that after I got rolling, when I'd hit a home run, Joe Simpson, one of the Braves broadcasters, kept saying, "Who is that? Javy or Gary Sheffield?"

Sheffield was our All-Star right fielder, and he was known throughout his career for hitting the ball very hard. And that's the way I was hitting it—hard!

I couldn't have asked for a better season than 2003. I only played in 129 games and had just 457 at-bats. What could I have done if I had played in 150 games? That's always been a question in my mind.

I had career highs in average (.328), home runs (43, fourth in the NL), RBIs (109, eighth), slugging percentage (.687), and on-base percentage (.378, fourth). I made the All-Star team, won the Silver Slugger, and finished fifth in voting for Most Valuable Player in the National League.

I always knew I was capable of putting up those kind of numbers. I just never had the patience. Those are the kind of numbers Mike Piazza put up, and I knew I was capable of that. Unfortunately, it took me 10 years before it happened. But I always knew I could do it.

Home runs were the big story for me in 2003. I averaged one home run every 10.6 at-bats, which was the second-best frequency in the NL after Barry Bonds (8.7). If I'd gotten 500 at-bats that year—which only happened in 2004 when I was with Baltimore—it is projected that my home run total would have been 47.

But because I was a catcher and played in Atlanta's heat and humidity, our manager Bobby Cox believed in giving me—and all the other starting catchers he had in his career—regular time off to keep us as fresh as possible.

In the end, it was my home runs that year that put me in the record book:

MOST HOME RUNS IN A SEASON, CATCHER
—Javy Lopez (42) 2003

The 42 isn't a typo. I did hit 43 home runs that season, but only 42 counted toward the record because one of my homers came as a pinch-hitter on July 20. The old record of 41 was set by the Mets' Todd Hundley in 1996.

Setting the home run record for catchers was a long shot for me because I usually didn't get that many at-bats. Also, Mike Piazza was playing in my era, and you could always count on him to hit 35 to 40 homers per year. I'm sure a lot more people expected him to break the record. He actually hit 40 home runs as a catcher twice—in 1997 with the Dodgers and in 1999 with the Mets. He had well over 500 at-bats both seasons, as he was the main guy in the lineup.

In 1996 Hundley played in 153 games and had 540 at-bats and 624 plate appearances (compared to my 129 games, 457 at-bats, and 495 plate appearances). He hit 41 home runs and had 112 RBIs with a .259 batting average.

When I reached 10 home runs on May 22, I wasn't thinking about a record, and I still wasn't thinking about it when I got to 20 on June 21. I put together a pretty good stretch at Turner Field in early June. I hit a home run against Texas on June 5. I didn't play the next day, and then I hit two home runs against Pittsburgh on June 7 and another one on June 8. After I hit that one, I got hit on the hand by a foul ball and almost came out of the game. But I decided to stay in, and I hit another home run in my last at-bat.

Two days in a row with two home runs, and five home runs in three games. I had eight games that year with two home runs, four of them in June within about a two-and-a-half-week period.

I also remember hitting two homers against the Phillies on June 24 when Kevin Millwood was pitching against us for the first time since the Braves traded him for Johnny Estrada, my backup catcher. I didn't have any idea about how that trade would eventually impact my career, but I found out that winter. We beat Millwood that day 5–3.

When I reached 30 as a catcher on August 8 with almost two months left in the season, I started thinking I had a good chance of breaking the record. That's when I began hearing comments from the media, people asking me, "Do you think you might be able to break the record for home runs by a catcher?"

I didn't even know what the record was. I just said, "I don't know. I'll continue to focus on what I'm doing, and if it happens, good. If it doesn't happen, I just want to finish the year putting up good numbers."

I remember a game against the Mets on September 3 in New York. It was miserable that day, raining nonstop and cold. I played the whole game, and we got beat 9–3.

But in the ninth inning, there were two outs, and we put in Estrada to pinch-hit. I was in the on-deck circle, and I told him to do me a favor: "Get on base. I'm going to hit one."

Johnny said, "No problem. I'll take care of you."

He got a hit, so I got a chance to bat again.

Sometimes players get a feeling that they're going to do something in a particular at-bat, and I did exactly what I had predicted. I hit one of my longest home runs ever at Shea Stadium, into the second deck. When I stepped on home plate, the first thing Estrada said was, "You owe me one."

I said, "Without a doubt!"

That was No. 35 as a catcher, No. 36 overall.

Well, it seemed like in a blink of an eye I was closing in on the record. I hit No. 38 as a catcher on September 10 in Atlanta off the Phillies' Vicente Padilla, and then No. 39 on September 13 at Florida off Dontrelle Willis, a left-hander who won the Rookie of the Year Award that year.

At that point, I was looking forward to setting the record. I told myself, "I'm not going to finish the season without breaking that record."

But it was tough. Because the end of the season was approaching, I was trying so hard—looking forward to hitting that one home run. The closer I got, though, the harder it seemed to get.

The home run to tie the record was pretty big, because once you tie the record, you're in the book. I hit it against the Marlins on September 20 at Turner Field in Atlanta. It came in the ninth inning off Braden Looper, a reliever. I hit a low pitch, a changeup or a splitter. I hit it almost off the ground and way out of the ballpark.

As soon as I hit it, the whole stadium exploded. That was a very, very emotional moment for me. I ended up coming out of the dugout to tip my cap and wave to the fans. There was a big crowd—more than 42,000. It was great for the Atlanta fans to be able to see me tie the record, and it was even better for me to feel the great support they gave me when I hit it.

When I tied the record, I was afraid it was going to take me too long to hit the next one because there weren't many games left. It took me a week. I hit it on September 27, the next-to-last day of the season. It's a good thing it didn't take me longer, or else the season would have been over! The record-breaker came against Amaury Telemaco, a big right-hander I hadn't done well against in the past. It was in the second inning with one out, no one on base, and a 2–0 count. As soon as I hit it I knew it was gone, and I flipped the bat, which is something I never did.

We had a 10-game lead in the standings. It was the next-to-last day of the season, and Bobby Cox could have put me on the bench to rest for the playoffs. But Bobby knew I was chasing the record, so he gave me the chance to do it, which I really appreciated.

When I hit that home run, it was a very happy moment. The Hall of Fame asked me for the bat I used for that record, and it is now in Cooperstown.

I felt a great sense of accomplishment when I set the record. At least I was in the record book. My name will be there until somebody breaks it—and somebody will break it someday. Records are made to be broken.

How long it will take, I don't know, but whoever breaks it will need to catch a lot of games. Any home runs hit as a pinch-hitter or a DH don't count toward the record, so that pretty much leaves out the catchers in the American League.

I noticed Hall of Famer Johnny Bench hit 45 home runs one year (1970 in 158 games, 605 at-bats, 671 PA), but he played outfield and first base, too. He caught 139 games, and only 38 of his home runs came when he was catching.

I'm very proud to have the record—very proud to be in the book. It was a big accomplishment for me, a kid from Ponce, Puerto Rico, who learned how to play baseball on a concrete basketball court in my neighborhood.

Most Home Runs by a Catcher in a Single Season
  42 **Javy Lopez, Braves** 2003
  41 Todd Hundley, Mets 1996
  40* Roy Campanella, Dodgers 1953
  40 Mike Piazza, Dodgers 1997
  40 Mike Piazza, Mets 1999
  38* Johnny Bench, Reds 1970
  36* Gabby Hartnett, Cubs 1930
  36 Mike Piazza, Dodgers 1996
  35 Walker Cooper, Giants 1947
  35 Mike Piazza, Dodgers 1993
  35 Ivan Rodriguez, Rangers 1999
  35 Mike Piazza, Mets 2000
  35* Johnny Bench, Reds 1972
  34 Terry Steinbach, A's 1996
  34 **Javy Lopez, Braves** 1998

* Hall of Famer

IN THE BEGINNING

I WAS BORN AND RAISED IN PONCE, THE SECOND-LARGEST CITY IN Puerto Rico, located on the south/central coast of the island. Among other things, Ponce has the main port on the Caribbean Sea.

Puerto Rico is a territory of the United States and is located between the Dominican Republic on the west and the Virgin Islands to the east.

Puerto Rican players coming out of high school and college are now eligible for the Major League Baseball draft, but that was not the case when I was coming out of high school. All Puerto Rican players were basically free agents at that time.

My dad, Jacinto Lopez, was a very hardworking man who had to support five kids. He worked in the auto parts business, and he also worked at a car dealership as a salesperson. Before I was born, he worked at a credit union.

My mom's name was Evelia Torres. That's why my name is Javier Lopez Torres. She had quite a few jobs. She worked in a bank and as a teacher, but at some point she had to leave all of that to take care of us.

I have one older brother and three sisters. My brother is Juan Eduardo Lopez, but everyone calls him Titico. My sisters are Sandra, Betsy, and Elaine. Elaine is the youngest of the five, and I am the second-youngest.

Sandra lives in Durango, Colorado, and Betsy lives in Ft. Lauderdale, Florida. Sandra left Puerto Rico when she was in her twenties. She got married, and her husband was in the air force. They moved to Germany and lived there for 15 years or so. Then they lived in Maryland, Texas, and Florida before settling in Colorado.

We're a close family. Maybe not as close as other families, but we stay in touch. Everyone is spread out. I frequently stay in touch with my dad and my brother, but only occasionally have contact with my sisters.

Since I retired, I usually go to Puerto Rico twice a year. But now with our baby, Brody, it's a little more complicated. But I always plan to spend New Year's Eve in Puerto Rico. It's a big deal.

My entire family gets together for a big party. We probably have about 50 people—all family—in my sister's house. We've got a pig on a spit, lots of drinks, lots of partying. It's a big tradition. At 4:00 in the morning, we're still going. It's a lot of fun. I really enjoy it.

We were a lower-middle-class family. We had a house with a mortgage. There were four little bedrooms. My parents had their room, of course, and my younger sister and I were in one room. My two older sisters lived in another room, and my brother had his own room. That was the setup, but they were all tiny rooms. There were two little bathrooms.

We had great neighbors with a lot of kids. Two of their kids and I were really into baseball, but I was more into it than anyone else. Everyone else played all sorts of games. Some were into basketball. It was a nice neighborhood. Good people. Good friends. Most were blue-collar, working-class families like ours.

The houses were very close together. We had a corner house, but we had a close neighbor on the back and also on one side. My dad still lives in the same house. Everybody in Ponce knows where he lives. He's by himself, but his twin sister, Lourdes, lives next door. I bought her house because her husband, who passed away a couple of years ago, had Alzheimer's and needed to be close by so my dad could help Lourdes take care of him. Eventually, they had no choice but to put him in a care facility, but my aunt still lives in that house next to my dad.

My dad is in his seventies now. He's not working, but he's in great shape, great health. But in 1999, when he was working for the newspaper as a distributor that took the papers to all the paperboys, he had a quadruple bypass. It was pretty bad, and I decided to take care of him financially so he wouldn't have to work. I told him, "This is it."

He'd been having chest pains. He was working too hard and had too much stress. My mom was also under a lot of stress because of how hard he was working, so I decided to take care of him. Ever since then, he hasn't worked—he's just been enjoying life. He usually comes to Atlanta to visit me at least once a year.

My mom was a very sweet lady. She passed away in 1999. When I started playing baseball, she was very supportive. She was at every game. But the older I got and the better I played, the more tense and exciting the games became, and she couldn't handle the excitement or the pressure.

Once I signed with the Braves, she hardly ever watched me hit because she was so nervous about what I was going to do. Even though she was so nervous watching me play, when I did well, she was the happiest person in the world. She came to quite a few games, including the 1995 World Series. My sister Elaine was with her, but my dad didn't come because he was working.

My mother was an excellent cook. I imagine everyone thinks their mom is the best cook in the world. She learned a lot from my dad's mom, who was an unbelievable cook. My grandmother liked to use a lot of wine in her food, kind of like Spanish dishes—a lot of wine and a lot of condiments. My mom was the same way. That's one reason my dad loved her so much—because she cooked like his mom!

My brother was an excellent basketball player in high school. He wasn't tall, but he was very quick and could jump. Unfortunately, he hung around in some bad company, and drugs took him away from basketball.

My two older sisters weren't much into sports, though Betsy was a decent volleyball player. But my younger sister, Elaine, was a very good volleyball player. She played for more than 20 years. She played for the Puerto Rican national team and went to Barcelona, Spain, for the 1992 Olympics and to Seoul, South Korea, for the 1988 Olympics.

Elaine is 5'10" and can really jump and hit hard. She was one of the shorter players on the Puerto Rican team, but she was one of the best spikers. And she hustles. She's everywhere. That's why she played so many years. She also played beach volleyball and traveled to a lot of different countries doing that.

Not too long ago, she decided to retire. She's still in unbelievable shape and could still play volleyball if she wanted to. Elaine opened a volleyball academy for girls and women in Dorado on the northern coast of Puerto Rico. Her husband is a lawyer. They're doing very well.

Elaine's first marriage was to former Texas Rangers star Juan Gonzalez, who hit 434 home runs from 1989 to 2005. When I tried to caution her against marrying Juan before they got married, it was like talking to a bat. She would not listen, and they weren't together long. A few years after that, she married Bertin, her husband now. I have to give him a lot of credit, because she has a very strong personality.

Betsy and her husband, Jesse Vassallo, are both swimming instructors in Ft. Lauderdale. Jesse was a very famous Puerto Rican swimmer, though he competed for the United States. He qualified for two Olympic teams (1980 and 1984) and was the first Puerto Rican to be inducted into the International Swimming Hall of Fame. He's held world records, and *Sports Illustrated* ranked him among the top 10 athletes in the world in 1979, along with Muhammad Ali and others.

I WAS A PAPERBOY FOR THREE YEARS, when I was 12, 13, and 14 years old. I delivered every morning, seven days a week, to about 25 houses, beginning around 4:00 or 5:00 in the morning. The last year, when I was 14, I was taking my dad's car instead of my bicycle. It was Puerto Rico—there are no rules down there!

It was a lot harder throwing the papers out of the car. It was a pain. I had to get in and out of the car a lot. It was easier on my bicycle, but it was a big deal for me to drive the car.

When I was 16 years old, I worked for the family of my future brother-in-law, Jesse Vassallo. His family owns Vassallo Industries, a company that manufactures products such as windows, doors, and PVC pipes. I was in the packaging area, where I put things in packages and taped them shut all day.

I only did that for three months because I was getting sick. They make the pipes there using some plastic chemical. Smelling that every day, I'd get a stomach ache and I wasn't hungry. It got to the point where it wasn't worth it. I got sick one day and didn't go back. It was a lot better being a paperboy.

Before I was a paperboy, my neighbor and I used to go door-to-door asking people if they needed their grass cut. I was 11 or 12 years old. They'd let us cut the grass and give us $2 or $3. My across-the-street neighbor had the biggest yard—the most work—but she paid the least. We'd get 50¢ or 75¢ and some candy, if we were lucky. I did it twice, and then I avoided her. If she called, I told everyone to tell her I wasn't there.

It was fun, though. I was always on my bicycle. I was the kind of kid that loved my bike. It wasn't the best-looking bike, but I was always riding it with my friends.

We had a lot of kids on my street, and one of the neighbors—Alejandro—and I used to make tape into a ball and use a broomstick for the bat. We'd keep score and play for hours like that. Sometimes I'd beat him, and sometimes he'd beat me.

I used to pretend I was some of the big-league stars—Reggie Jackson, Jack Clark, George Foster. I always tried to be one of those guys. Dave Winfield, too. It was fun. When I was Reggie Jackson, I'd bat left-handed. But I was only good batting right-handed.

Alejandro and I decided to get into cockfighting, too. Another boy named Stephen—he and his brother, Joe, are the ones who invited me to play baseball for the first time in my life—used to have roosters and chickens at their house, and they gave me my first rooster. They had five or six on their patio, and Stephen gave me one to take home. I didn't have a cage or anything, so I made a little place where I thought it couldn't get out, and I put a lot of corn around so he would stay there and eat it.

I hoped he wouldn't run away at night, but he wound up in the mango tree in the backyard and started crowing when the sun came up. The next day, he wound up where he used to be—four houses down the road at Stephen's. Stephen called and said, "Javy, your rooster came back to my house. You better get a cage or something."

That was the first time I had a rooster, and I picked up the rooster "bug." Alejandro and I used to go to this cockfight. It's legal in Puerto Rico, but we couldn't get in because we were minors. But we could see the fights a little through the walls at the arena or dome where they held them. We liked to be around the area where all the roosters were being treated and fed and trained. It was like a zoo, walking and seeing all these roosters. It was fascinating.

When a rooster loses, a lot of times, they kill it. I remember this guy whose rooster was winning, but then it lost when the other rooster made a lucky kick and hit it in the neck. The owner was about to kill it, but when he came outside the dome, I told him I'd take it.

The poor rooster's face was swollen from the fight. But I took it home, cleaned it, fed it, and put it in the cage, because the other rooster Stephen had given me had died. I had taken him out of the cage, and I couldn't catch him, and later I think a cat or two got him.

Each day I'd clean my new rooster and feed him, and in about a week, you could see he was getting better and better and better. I asked another guy if he had a hen I could have. The rooster lived happily ever after.

I started getting more chickens and roosters. There was a time when I had about 10 in the backyard. As I got older, I wasn't taking good care of them because I was into other things, so my dad told me to get rid of them. When I married my first wife, her dad was into raising roosters, and I used to go to the cockfights with him.

My dad used to play for a baseball team, but he just played for fun—recreational, never professional. I guess he was a decent player, but I didn't see him play. I think he played the outfield.

He had this baseball bat in the closet for many years, and one day I decided to use it. He didn't want me to use it at first, but then he said he didn't mind as long as I took care of it. Of course, I broke it. So, I put some nails in it and wrapped tape around it. I told him it was to give the bat a better grip. I don't think he ever found out that the bat was broken.

I'VE BEEN PLAYING BASEBALL SINCE I WAS ABOUT SEVEN YEARS OLD. Four houses down the street, there was a church. These people created a church at their house. The two guys who lived there—Stephen and Joe Cordero—put together a team to play baseball.

I had no idea what baseball was all about. I had never heard of the game. They said, "We'll teach you how to play."

So we went to a concrete basketball court to play. The infield was concrete, but the outfield was the grass area off the court. We had a rubber ball, and I said, "What am I supposed to do?" The only sport I knew was basketball.

They began to teach me how to play baseball. They said, "If the ball is in the air and you catch it, it's an out. If the ball is on the ground, you catch it and throw to that guy over there—first base—before the runner gets there. You have to get three outs."

Like I said, I didn't know the first thing about baseball. I just said, "Okay. Then what?"

They told me, "We go and hit. The pitcher throws the ball. You hit it, and you've got to run."

I remember the first time I hit the ball, I ran straight to second base. They yelled, "No! No! You've got to touch first base first, then second, then third and home to score!" I was only seven years old. Even big-leaguers have to start somewhere!

When I was eight years old, I was just playing baseball with the kids in the neighborhood. I started to get the feeling for it and was playing more often. I was enjoying the game, so my dad decided to take me to a rec league tryout in Ponce when I was nine.

We went to the tryouts one day, and I played catch. They needed one more guy, and when they saw me playing catch, they must have seen my potential. Two days later, they told my dad, "Your son made the team."

The name of the team was the Criollos. In English, that would be the Spartans. Strong. If you are a Criollo, you're from the country, from Puerto Rico—a native.

The coaches saw I had a pretty good arm and tried me first as a pitcher. I didn't know anything about pitching. I just started throwing as hard as I could, but I was hitting kids. I was kind of embarrassed, because every time I hit a kid, he started crying.

Everyone kept telling me, "Throw at the catcher!"

I was doing that, but I kept seeing kids going to first base. I said, "What's happening?"

The coaches said, "You've got to throw in this area," and one of them outlined an area with his hands—like the strike zone, though I didn't know about that yet.

The catcher was a little chubby guy, and when he squatted down, I felt like I had to throw the ball into the ground to get a strike. That first day I played was a real experience—hitting guys, walking people, and I had no clue what I was doing.

After a while, my dad took me to a park to practice. He was taller, and I was regularly hitting the strike zone when I was pitching to him. But once I had to throw to that little guy again, it was like throwing into the dirt.

I must have looked pretty hopeless because they decided to move me to shortstop. They were hitting the ball hard, right at me, and I was trying to field it sideways. I might as well have been saying "Olé!" like a bullfighter stepping aside to let the bull pass through the cape.

That didn't work out either, so I ended up in the outfield, which was kind of hard, too. They'd hit a fly ball and I'd start running forward, but then I'd see the ball going over my head, and I'd have to start running back.

They couldn't find a position where I didn't embarrass myself, but my hitting was good. I was hitting the ball hard. The problem was I didn't have any defensive skills.

It took me another year to learn those. I watched a lot of baseball, and I learned a lot. As soon as the Criollos' season was over, my dad put me on a different team right away. Baseball is played all year in Puerto Rico because the weather is so good. I gained a lot more experience on my second team because I knew what I was doing and I knew what the game was all about. I just tried to get better.

It was on my third team that I really thought I was making progress in learning how to play baseball.

It was about that time that I suffered my first baseball injury. I broke my wrist. When I wasn't playing with my rec-league team, I was playing with the neighborhood kids on the basketball court. There was some sort of construction or landscaping going on, and they left a pile of dirt. When I was going back to catch the ball, I hit the pile of dirt and fell backward. I guess it was sort of like playing center field in Houston today, where they have that grassy mound.

The rec league was starting, but I couldn't play because my arm was in a cast. I decided to sign up with a different subdivision so I could play. They signed me even though I still had the cast on. I played with Glenview Garden, and that's when my career kind of took off. My confidence, the way I played…it was like I suddenly flipped the switch. I was 11 years old. That year I hit around 15 home runs with the All-Star team when we played against different subdivisions in the town. Every year I was getting better and better and better.

I was an outfielder at the beginning. Then they put me at shortstop. Then at the age of 13 they decided to try me as a catcher. Our catcher got hurt during practice and we didn't have another one. There was a substitute catcher, but he was also one of our best pitchers. The coaches tried me at catcher in practice, and that's how it began. I kind of liked wearing the gear and everything.

When I tried on the gear the first time, they said, "Throw a few to second base," and I gunned it down to second every time. They had simulated runners at first trying to steal, and I was throwing them out.

That weekend was my first game. Every once in a while, I'd drop a ball. I couldn't block. A lot of times the pitcher would throw a bad pitch that got past me, but the backstop was only about five feet behind me. I'd pick up the ball and still throw out the guy at second. That day, I threw out quite a few guys, and after the game, the manager said, "Welcome to your new position!" After that day, I never played shortstop or the outfield or pitcher for him again.

The manager was Johnny Rodriquez. He's still around. He lives in Ponce. He's probably still telling people about making a catcher out of me. I know he tells people he was my manager for two or three years.

When I was growing up, baseball was a big passion in Puerto Rico. There were three big sports—basketball, volleyball, and baseball. A lot of kids dreamed of becoming a Major League Baseball player, but that really wasn't my goal. I guess I was playing baseball because I loved the game. I never, ever thought about making it to the big leagues.

I didn't start thinking about the big leagues until I was 15 or 16 years old, and then it was only because of all the comments I started hearing from people. "You're going to be in the big leagues!" and stuff like that. Before that, I just played for fun and because I loved it. I never thought I'd be a major league player.

I DID WATCH SOME OF THE BIG-LEAGUE GAMES. One of my heroes growing up was Jose Cruz, who lived about a half hour from where we lived in Ponce. He was an outfielder for the Cardinals, Astros, and Yankees from 1970 to 1988. He had a .284 career batting average with 165 home runs and 317 stolen bases. He made two All-Star teams and won two Silver Sluggers.

I remember one time in Los Caobos, the neighborhood where I first played baseball, he came with his two brothers, Tommy and Hector Cruz, who both played in the big leagues too. They came over to do clinics.

I'm sure my mouth was hanging open listening to them because I was so excited about what they were saying. At the end, they gave me a baseball signed by all three of them. My dad still has that ball.

One time my dad took me with him when he was selling auto parts out of his van. We were near Arroyo, where Jose Cruz lived. We drove by his house and he was outside, so my dad decided to stop. I was very embarrassed. I didn't want my dad to stop at a celebrity's house and introduce me.

But Jose was the nicest person. He started talking to my dad like he'd known him forever. And then he started talking to me. One of his sons was out there, and I was playing with him—it was his older son, not Jose Jr., who played 12 years in the big leagues.

I was blown away by the fact that Jose was there talking to us and giving me advice. He told me things like, "This is a passion. You have to eat and sleep with it. You have to work hard and have a passion for it." And that's the way approached it from then on.

Ever since I was 11 years old, I've had a passion for baseball. I remember how I always looked forward to practice during the week. I used to go to this public school, and after school, I had to walk home. It took me almost 40 minutes. I walked all the way home and then had to go to practice.

A few times, I got to practice late because I had to walk home from school, then get dressed, and then wait for my dad to take me. I decided I didn't want to be late again, so the days I had practice, I put my practice uniform on and then put the school uniform on top of it. I was burning up in school. It was hot—90 degrees—but I didn't care. I was ready for practice!

I showed the other kids: "Look, here are my stirrups." It was funny. My glove was in my book bag, and that's how I'd go to school every day I had practice. I always looked forward to it. I wanted to be the first one there.

The first school I went to was a private school that my grandma put me in. I was only there for kindergarten. Then I went to a public school called Tomas Carreon Maduro, and I was there for four years. I was playing basketball too and was pretty decent at it.

The basketball rec team I was on was playing at a place called La Playa, and the coach was a PE teacher at a private school called San Judas Tadeo. He liked me and talked to the people at the school, and they gave me a partial scholarship to play basketball.

I started there in the fifth grade, and I began playing volleyball there too. I actually became a better volleyball player than a basketball player.

I was at that school from fifth grade until ninth grade. Then in the ninth grade, another school, Academia Cristo Rey, gave me a partial scholarship—this time for volleyball. Baseball was always played outside the school. That was typical in Puerto Rico. There were some schools with baseball fields, but there were no leagues. Teams just played among themselves.

I was named Ponce's Athlete of the Year three straight years in high school, but I didn't really think much about it. There wasn't any presentation or trophy or anything like that.

My last year of rec ball was when I was 15 years old, and I hit around .500 with a bunch of home runs. That's when I saw my first scout.

My dad decided to take me to a tryout that a prep school was doing in my hometown. It was a Christian school from Alabama. At 15 years old, I was hitting the ball out of the stadium, and no one else was doing that.

After the tryout, the whole crew from that school came over to my house to talk to my dad. They had a translator with them. At the beginning, I was interested in that school in Alabama. They told my dad there would be a lot of scouts there and that I would be in professional baseball in no time. My dad was kind of excited. But I got cold feet. I read the pamphlet, and I thought, *Alabama? A 15-year-old in Alabama?*

When it was time to decide if I wanted to go or not, I decided not to go. Instead, I played Youth AA. You have to be selected to play Youth AA. They give you a few dollars for "meal money," and you play against teams from the other cities in Puerto Rico.

When I started playing Youth AA at age 16, the first scout that watched me was from the San Diego Padres. He happened to be there that day because after my game was the Big AA—17-year-olds. He was there to see a couple of kids he was interested in, but my game was before that, so he watched me, and I happened to be raking that day.

He decided to talk to my dad. The scout's name was Abraham Martinez, and he actually signed Sandy Alomar for the Padres. He was wearing a Padres polo shirt, and he told my dad he really was interested in me and gave him his business card. After the game, I came over to shake his hand. He said, "You've got a lot of talent."

I hit at least one home run in that game, maybe two. I had a great game. I had no idea he was back there or who he was or what he was doing. I thought he was a coach or something.

After that day, every time I played I looked in the stands to see if there were any scouts. The following year when I played Youth AA, I started to see two or three scouts at every single game. I got pumped up. Every time I played, there was a new scout approaching my dad. At least 15 teams, maybe more, were watching me.

A lot of teams called my house. I was overwhelmed. Every day when I came home from school, my dad would say, "The Astros called…the Yankees called…San Diego…the Dodgers called."

They all talked about being interested, but none said anything about signing bonuses. No one did that until I was almost 17, the age when I could sign.

At 16 years old, my first year of Youth AA, I was supposed to be on the bench, because the guy who was the starting catcher had already been there for a year.

We started playing exhibition games, though, and I was hitting the ball really well. They said, "You've got to be in the lineup." So I started in the outfield. But we played two games. One game I was in the outfield, and the other game I was the catcher.

Our starting catcher—Ricky Maldonado—had a cannon of an arm and wound up signing with the Expos. We played against each other in Bradenton, Florida.

He didn't play any other position, but one game he pitched because he had such a great arm, and I was the catcher. It was fun catching him because he had a great curveball and a great fastball. I don't think he got above Class A as a pro. He didn't have the best work habits and decided to quit. He took himself out.

After that, my hitting was outstanding. The rest of that year, I'd catch every other game, and he would either pitch that game or be at first base because they needed his bat in the lineup. I was in left field when I wasn't catching.

The Braves didn't see me play that first year at age 16. None of the Braves scouts came to my games. Then one day, my dad and I decided to go to a tournament in the San Juan–Bayamon area in the north of Puerto

Rico. It's about an hour and 20 minutes from Ponce. I was watching the game because Ricky Maldonado was playing.

There were a lot of scouts there. I shook hands with some of the scouts who I'd already talked to. And then this guy I hadn't seen came over, and it happened to be Jorge Posada, father of the future Yankees catcher. He introduced himself.

"I'm a scout for the Braves," he said. "I haven't seen you play, but I've heard nothing but good things about you. We're very, very interested. Here's my card. We're going to check on you next year."

I was just 16. I guess he took advice from other people about what type of player I was. We stayed in touch, and I thought, *The Braves! Wow! TBS!*

That's the first time I saw Posada, and the following year he came and watched me play any time I was in that area. He kept in touch with my dad, and he's the first scout who started offering money. Nobody else was talking about money at that point.

At that time, Benito Santiago, a catcher from Ponce, was my inspiration. In 1987 he had a great rookie year with San Diego when he batted .300 and was National League Rookie of the Year and even won the Silver Slugger. He was in every magazine. He was the highlight of the year. I wanted to be like Benito.

I couldn't be like Jose Cruz, because he was an outfielder. I wanted to be like Benito. He was my idol. Jose was my idol as a complete player, and Benito was my idol as a catcher.

The rule was that I had to wait until my 17th birthday—November 5, 1987—to sign. To be completely honest, I signed a few months earlier than I should have and continued to play, even though I had signed. That was supposed to be illegal. If you sign with a professional team, you're not supposed to keep playing youth ball. You're a professional. Once you sign, you can't play the rest of the amateur league. But I continued playing, and scouts kept coming after me because no one knew for sure that I had signed. I'm sure there were a few scouts who suspected something was wrong.

After I signed but before it was announced, Bobby Cox came from Atlanta to Puerto Rico to see me play in one of the games I technically should not have been playing in. I had no idea then who Bobby Cox was.

He was the Braves general manager at the time. He actually watched me twice, and I didn't even know he was there. My dad was all excited, though.

Still, on my 17th birthday, there were quite a few teams waiting. San Diego, the Dodgers, the Yankees, and the rest of them. Of course, wouldn't you know it that once I'd already signed with the Braves, the rest of the teams came in and started offering me a lot more money? I thought I was having trouble trying to get a good contract. Then all these other ones came along!

But I said, "You know what? Forget it! I'm going to be in Atlanta, on TBS."

My dad was the one having a hard time. Like any other dad, he wanted the most for his kid. I got $37,000. I know the Expos went to $50,000. I think the most I got offered was $90,000, but I'm not sure what team it was, maybe San Diego. That was a lot of money in 1987.

My dad was embarrassed about signing for relatively little money, but it was because I told him, "I want to sign! I want to sign with the Braves!"

I decided to sign with the Braves for a couple reasons. First, looking around the big leagues at that time, Ozzie Virgil was the Braves catcher, and I think he was 30 in 1987. So I thought by the time I made it to the big leagues, he'd probably be retired. I didn't know how long it was going to take me.

But the main reason I picked the Braves was TBS. I wanted to make sure my family could see me play on TV all the time.

When I finally made the announcement public on my birthday, my dad wanted to be sure I said I signed for $90,000, instead of $37,000. I had to lie! All the papers said, "Javy Lopez signs $90,000 contract with Braves!" My dad even talked to Posada and told him, "Make sure you tell everyone it was $90,000."

Posada was just a typical scout. He said that $37,000 was all the Braves could afford. But they also signed an outfielder named Melvin Nieves that year. I had come up with Melvin, and when I asked him how much he got, he told me he got a $100,000 signing bonus. My heart just dropped when I heard that.

Posada was telling me I had gotten one of the highest bonuses ever by the Braves. Yeah, right! At the same time, what made me feel a lot better was talking to these Dominican guys. They got maybe a $1,000 signing bonus. Some just got a pair of batting gloves or a glove and bat. I thought, *Look at them. They got nothing. I got $37,000 at least.*

Most of my bonus money went to pay off the mortgage on my dad's house. And I bought myself a used car, a red Honda Prelude. I loved it. It was my first car and cost $4,000. It had about 40,000 miles on it. It was a good-looking car.

The only problem was it was a 1984, and this was 1987, and it didn't have an air conditioner. I thought I'd buy it and put one in—but I couldn't find one. I had to ride in that car for two or three years without air conditioning. When I was in traffic, the engine heated up. Eventually I got rid of it and bought a Honda Accord—with an air conditioner, of course.

I loved the Accord. With the little money I was making at that time, I painted it and put on a spoiler and new wheels. But where I lived, I had to leave my car outside. In the middle of the night, some people just ripped off the spoiler that was on top of the trunk. And they took the wheel covers.

Then the car looked so ugly—two holes on top of the trunk where the spoiler had been, and no wheel covers. So, I took it to the body shop and decided to cover the holes—no spoiler. And I bought a new set of wheels with no caps so they couldn't steal anything. The car didn't look the same, but at least there wasn't anything to steal!

THE MELTDOWN

WHEN I SIGNED WITH THE BRAVES IN 1987, I WAS STILL A SENIOR IN high school. During spring break in 1988, we were off the whole week for Semana Santa—holy week. So, along with Melvin Nieves, an outfielder from Puerto Rico who had also just signed with the Braves, I was able to go to spring training for the week and get a feel for it. We took a plane to West Palm Beach, Florida.

We flew from Puerto Rico to Miami, and from Miami we took a little plane to West Palm Beach. That was the first time I experienced a small plane, but I wasn't that nervous. I'd just signed and I wasn't married. I guess when you're younger, you're fearless. The older you get, the more you've got in life, the more fear you have.

But Melvin Nieves' dad was shaking he was so scared on the second flight to West Palm Beach. After a week, we went back to Puerto Rico, then flew to Miami again for the summer after finishing high school. This time, I went from Puerto Rico to Miami and from Miami to Bradenton—Pirates City. That's where the Braves had their extended spring training for the minor league system. I took another "knuckle ball" airplane. That's what I called the small planes because of the way they danced around.

I didn't know Melvin before that first flight other than having played against him a few times. He knew who I was, but I didn't know who he was. On the plane, he was talking like he'd known me forever. To me, he was like someone I just met. We were talking about playing Little League against each other a few times, and once we landed in West Palm Beach, I realized he was with the Braves too. He was my teammate. I knew someone. I wasn't by myself.

I didn't know what to expect when we got there. I didn't know if there was just one field. Was there going to be a group of kids like me? That's what I was expecting. When I got there, I saw a whole complex with 10 fields and 200 to 300 players. I thought, *Holy shit! What is this?*

I'd been telling my dad, "You know what? I'll spend a year in the minor leagues and go to the big leagues quick." But when I got there, it was like, "Hello! Welcome to the world!"

I was very impressed. We had a meeting the first day, and it was a big blow for me. I didn't know any English. I learned English after I signed, throughout my career. I got there and had to stand next to a Spanish-speaking coach so he could translate everything the other coach was saying: "This is the program. This is what we're going to do. Blah, blah, blah."

I remember we all met on one of the fields at 9:00 AM—200 players on one field. One of the coaches was talking—loudly. Among the coaches was Rick Albert. He's been a coach in the Braves' farm system for a long time. The guy translating for me was Pedro Gonzalez, a coach who was a former second baseman in the big leagues. Gil Garrido, another coach who played in the big leagues, was helping me with the translating too.

At the beginning, I didn't think the language would be a big thing. I thought I could learn it. But then they told me, "You are the catcher. You need to communicate. You need to scream. You need to let them know you are the main guy on the field. You need to speak loud."

It was embarrassing for me to scream in my poor English.

For example: "First and third!"

It was impossible for me to say "first." It came out "Fir...fir...fir..."

It was hard. My first year was in Bradenton in the rookie Gulf Coast League, and all my roommates were Spanish-speaking players. My second year, I started in Bradenton for extended spring training, and then I went to Pulaski, Virginia, to play with the rookie team in the Appalachian League. I had Melvin Nieves as a roommate at Pulaski, but he and I had a confrontation. It was my fault. I guess I drank his orange juice in the morning. I just took a cup of it, but there was a big fight. "You've got to give me money for that," he said. Of course, I was pretty sure he was drinking my juice, too.

He was making rules, and I said, "You're not my dad, and you're not my ma. This is my room. Leave me alone. There are no rules. I can come here and leave here anytime I want." Anyway, there were some issues with him, so I decided to leave and chose an American roommate. At the beginning, the American roomie wasn't too crazy about it, but then he realized I was another guy who could help pay the rent.

The guy's name was Walter Roy. He was a right-handed pitcher from Detroit. I was with him in Pulaski. It was him and Darren Ritter, a big right-handed pitcher from Baltimore. I had to learn English living with them. Walter's wife was there too. She was a very sweet lady, and she talked to me all the time, taught me a lot.

And wouldn't you know it, Melvin Nieves moved in with a group of guys right next door!

After that, I tried to pick an American roomie every year so I could try to learn the language. I was with Walter Roy again in 1990. I had had a great time with him the year before, so I decided to room with him again. That was in Burlington, Iowa.

I still feel awful about something that happened in Burlington on an off day. We were playing basketball, and it was cold. It was always cold there! I got a rebound and swung my arms. Roberto Deleon, a left-handed pitcher, was trying to get the ball behind my back, and I snapped his finger and broke it. It was the end of the season for him, and he'd been pitching well: 3–1 with a 2.45 ERA in relief at the time.

I felt so guilty. I didn't try to do it on purpose. He was trying to get the ball from behind me…and *craaack!*

We had to come up with an excuse—he slammed his finger in the door or some lie—that we could tell our manager, Jim Saul, the next day. That night we had to take him to the hospital. The bone was out of the skin. They had to perform surgery. He never really could pitch again. I feel awful about that.

The other thing I think of when I think of Burlington is all the passed balls I had—31! That's too many. Do you know why? It was about 10 degrees! I was afraid to catch the ball. And at 10 degrees, the pitchers don't have the grip—they're throwing all over the place. It was so cold!

At Durham in 1991, I was going to live with Walter Roy again, but he got released.

Then that May in Durham, I got married, and I had my own place with my wife at the time, Analy. She was from Ponce. I met her in the ninth grade when she came over from a different school.

In 1992 I went to Double A at Greenville, South Carolina. In Greenville, my wife and I shared a place with a pitcher from Puerto Rico named Marcos Vasquez and his wife. He and his wife were very good friends of ours, and we got a place together to try and save money on the rent. It was a three-bedroom apartment, and we had another guy with us. That was Ramon Caraballo, an infielder who eventually spent a little time in the majors.

After the incident with Nieves, these were my first Spanish-speaking roommates, but my English was a lot better by then.

After that, I always had my own place. In Triple A, I met Paul Kinzer. He's an agent now, but back then he was a guy who helped a lot of players by setting them up for signings and card shows. When I got called up to Atlanta from Triple A in 1992 and again in 1993, he allowed me to stay at his house. He lives in Douglasville, just south of Atlanta. He and his family are just awesome people. We're still in touch.

THE LANGUAGE BARRIER HAS BEEN A CHALLENGE THROUGHOUT MY CAREER. If it wasn't for that, I could have been more of a leader. But I was always afraid to talk because of the mistakes I might make. I get embarrassed very easily. To avoid that, I decided it was better not to say anything.

A lot of times, the leader on the field is the catcher. In my situation, I just couldn't be it. There was something in the back of my head that wouldn't allow me to just break that barrier and say, "Forget it. If you make a mistake, the heck with it."

When I signed with the Orioles in 2004, it was a totally different crew—different team, coaches, and players. I was more confident and outgoing. I knew a lot of the young players, so I felt obligated to be their mentor. We had veterans there like B.J. Surhoff and Rafael Palmeiro, guys with a lot more years playing than me. So I still wasn't as much of a leader as I could have been.

The language barrier was tough in the minor leagues. It was embarrassing. A lot of times, I went to eat with the other players, the American players. When it was time to order breakfast, I'd say, "Eggs, pancakes."

The waitress would ask, "Do you want hash browns with that?"

I had no idea what hash browns were, but I said, "Yes."

Then she asked, "Do you want your eggs medium, over easy, or scrambled?"

She would have to show me pictures of it. Some of the other players would start laughing, and I'd be thinking, *Oh, no...*

It was embarrassing. I had to point to the picture of how I wanted my eggs—scrambled.

When I ordered steak for dinner, they'd ask, "How do you want it cooked? Medium, medium-well…"

I had no idea.

When I ordered salad, they asked what kind of dressing…"Balsamic vinaigrette, Caesar…"

Again, I had no idea.

One time at Pulaski in 1989, I had to order at the drive-thru window at McDonald's. This American guy, a catcher named Sean Hutchinson, was in front of me, so I told him what to order for me.

"I want the loose—the loose."

He's like, "What? What?"

And the lady said, "Can I take your order?"

I said, "Yeah, the loose, the loose, the big de-loose."

They're like, "What number?"

"No. 5."

It was the Big Deluxe!

Steve and another guy were cracking up. That became the talk of the team. All the American guys started calling me "Big De-Loose."

That incident probably kept me from talking more for years after that. I just decided not to talk much. Even Melvin Nieves would crack up when I made a mistake. I said, "Dude, you slur English and make mistakes too."

But he was still making fun of the way I talked.

I don't think it ever impacted the way I played, though. I totally ignored everything once the game started. After the game or before the game, I just had to take it the way it was. I always said to myself, "People can make fun of me as much as they want."

I had two rules. If somebody broke those rules, then they were in trouble with me. One was, don't say something about my parents or my family. Make fun of me as much as you want, but once you mention my parents, that's it. The other thing was, don't touch me. Say whatever you want about me, but once you put a hand on me, then we have issues. As long as it's just talking about me, that's okay. I can be their clown or whatever. "As long as you guys are happy," I said.

Once the game started, I played *my* game. That's it. Otherwise, I'd have been out of baseball. I couldn't let all that stuff get into my head.

There's a lot of envy. A lot of people would have liked to see me fail. I just had to ignore all of that.

I've told my kids the same thing. There are bullies in school. Javy, my older son, is 15 years old. There aren't many Latin guys in his school, so this American guy has been all over him. Javy said the kid kept calling him an illegal immigrant.

I said, "Javy, you know what? Ignore it. But if he touches you or says something about your brother or your family, then…"

It's inevitable that kids are going to experience these things. You can tell the principal, and the principal might take care of that kid, but then somebody else will come along. There's always somebody else. Sometimes you just have to live with it.

GRADY LITTLE WAS MY MANAGER FOR THREE YEARS in the minor leagues: 1991 at Durham, 1992 at Greenville, and 1993 at Richmond. He pretty much gave me the hope that someday I would be a major leaguer. He gave me the confidence. Our chemistry was good. That's why I played so well.

It was enjoyable to play for Grady, who later managed four years in the majors for the Red Sox and Dodgers, and that's a big reason why I played so well for him. Because of that, I was able to step up among all the promising catchers the Braves had when I signed.

Grady especially helped me with my attitude. Before 1991 I was playing uptight, scared. You can tell by the numbers. I was too anxious to get better, working too hard to make progress. He loosened me up.

Before I signed with the Braves, I was hitting for a really high average with a lot of home runs. Of course, that wasn't pro ball. After signing, I hit one home run my first year and three my second year. I knew that wasn't me. I knew I was better than that.

I wasn't happy, and it was keeping me from getting better. I was uptight and frustrated, because I wasn't putting up the numbers. Grady is a gambler. He believes you don't know what you can do until you try.

He told me, "If you're going to strike out, make sure you strike out with authority. Swing hard in case you hit it. If you want to throw someone out at second base, throw hard in case you make a good throw. But don't throw easy just to try to put it on top of the base.

"If that's not your style, don't do it. Be you. Play relaxed. Laugh. If you make a mistake, who cares? The only way you're not going to make mistakes is not to play baseball at all. Because everyone who plays baseball makes mistakes."

The first year I played for him was Durham in the advanced Class A Carolina League. It was tough. I hit 11 home runs, but I only batted .245. I wasn't good offensively, and the team wasn't that great. Actually, we were 79–58, which isn't bad, but we still finished third in the division.

I made the Carolina League All-Star team, but that was because the rest of the catchers in the league were doing worse than I was. I went to the All-Star Game four years in a row in the minors.

But I wasn't happy at all. My wife at the time had to go back to Puerto Rico so she could finish college, and I had to stay another month in Durham to finish the season.

I was trying everything—getting there early, practicing, but nothing worked. That's because it was all in my head.

I remember with three days left in the season, I had a big meltdown. I went to my room and started crying. It seemed like I cried all night. I thought, *Why is this happening to me? I gave everything I've got. Why?*

I guess the meltdown helped in the long run. I never thought about quitting, but I actually was afraid the Braves were going to release me, that I was going to disappoint my dad, my mom. I wouldn't be able to support my wife. What was I going to do if I didn't play baseball? That was what I loved to do. I didn't want to do anything else.

I was afraid. I cried, I prayed, and then I went to sleep and woke up in the morning saying, "It's a new day." I went back to the ballpark, and I guess I was happy because the season was almost over. When you're not doing well, the season can be very, very long.

I played better after the meltdown. I started hitting the ball the opposite way. Whatever I did clicked. I remember my first at-bat the next day. I hit a really hard line drive to right field. Even though the guy caught it, I felt good because it was an outside pitch, and I went to right field and hit the crap out of the ball. It was a perfect swing.

I was trying to do exactly the same thing every at-bat after that. There were only two more days left after that—and one of the days I didn't play. The last day, I went 0-for-4, but I hit the ball hard, solid, kind of letting the Braves know what I could really do.

The year was over. I went back to Puerto Rico and played winter ball for the San Juan Senators. I was trying to maintain what I had learned in Durham, and I got better. I wasn't playing every day, but on the bench, I decided to watch all these players and see what they were doing and try to copy the good and leave the bad.

I played winter ball for nine years, from 1988 to 1996. I stopped playing because, as a catcher, it's a long season in the big leagues—spring training and then the season and playoffs—and it's tough to then go to Puerto Rico and continue catching.

I'd much rather spend the winter with family, enjoy Christmas with them, and prepare myself for the following season. At the same time, I know a lot of people wanted to see me play all the time.

But if I had gotten hurt playing winter ball, that could have affected my career in the big leagues. They said, "All these Dominican guys play winter ball." Yeah, and they're lucky they didn't get hurt. Once you get hurt, that's it. Winter ball is not going to pay your salary.

For me, it was more important to spend time with the family. You're always on the road during the season. You only have three and a half months before going back to spring training. I would have rather spent that time with my family and seen my kids growing.

The following year at Greenville—1992—is when we had that tremendous team. We had a few different players than at Durham, but it was pretty much the same team. Just another year at a higher level. We really clicked that year, though.

I felt I was able to carry everything through to 1992 in Double A. And I saw a big difference in Grady's approach to the players that season. He was nice to the players all year long—of course, it helped that we were winning. But the reason we were winning was that he was inspirational for us from the start of the season.

His approach to the team was completely different than it had been in Durham. Every day when we came to the clubhouse, there was a new motivational message written on the board.

That opened a lot of minds and made the players more relaxed and confident. That's a big reason why we won 106 games, including the playoffs, and lost only 45. We won the Southern League championship and had a .702 winning percentage. That team is considered one of the best minor league teams of all time.

In 1993 at Richmond in Triple A, Grady pretty much kept the same thing going. He works on the psychological part of the players, the players' brains. He works on your head, which is so important, because 70 to 80 percent of baseball is mental, and Grady was good at getting in people's heads.

I was with Chipper Jones the second half of 1992 at Greenville and with him and Ryan Klesko in 1993 at Triple A. Chipper (first round, 1990) and Klesko (fifth round, 1989) were top draft picks, so they were always sent to the better team every year. I was always going to the "*B* team," so I didn't play with them until Double A and Triple A, where there's just one team.

I hadn't seen them play until we were on the same team, but I'd heard a lot about them. Chipper was very impressive. He was a hitting machine, not only for power, but also for consistency.

Klesko was a power hitter all the time, and when Grady said, "strike out with authority"—that was Klesko. It might look like he was about to break his back, but he was going to be sure he got a good hack at it, whether he hit it or not.

They were both impressive hitters. I got to know Klesko more than Chipper, because Klesko and I stayed with Paul Kinzer. He and I hung out a lot.

Chipper was a different story. He was a first-round pick, and everybody wanted to be around him. He had his own entourage!

But Klesko and I got to know each other really well, and you'll read a lot more about our experiences later. I got to know his parents. They're very interesting people. Ryan lives in Macon. He's got property everywhere. I like him a lot, but he's still a knucklehead! He's so involved in so many things—hunting, surfing—I heard he's into making coffee now.

At spring training in 1992, I got some great advice from a player named Jeff Manto. He was with Richmond, but he watched me in batting practice and took me aside and gave me a few tips—elbow closed, always think to the middle. I forget all the things he said—but after that, I did exactly what he told me, and my hitting really took off.

I went to Double A that year and was the league's MVP. I hit .321 and ended up in the big leagues in September. The next year, I hit .305 at Richmond and ended up in the big leagues again.

Manto has no idea how much impact his tips had on me. That was his only year in the Braves organization. He was mainly a third baseman, and he played 289 games in the big leagues with eight teams. Now he's the minor league hitting coordinator for the White Sox, so I guess he knew what he was talking about. I just took his advice, and I've never forgotten what it did for me.

My first day in Greenville, I naturally noticed it was a bigger stadium with more people, so I knew I was stepping up. It was a good motivational start for me, knowing that I was in a bigger place—more media, things like that.

Then the season opened, and we were winning, and I started playing well. I usually don't look at my batting average or anything. But the first month, I was doing so well that I decided to look at the stat sheet, not just for my team but for the whole league. I saw I was first in batting average, and I thought, *First place...okay! Awesome.*

I was leading the league in average, and I had to maintain. Every day, I was working even harder in batting practice.

It was a fun season. Grady Little with his quotes, the team was winning, and everybody was getting along. All that combined just made me more excited about playing baseball. You put all these things together, and for anyone who plays baseball, that is the perfect year.

You don't want to play baseball just to play. You want to play with a team where you feel happy, where you get along with all the players. If you love baseball and play with a team where you don't like the manager and there are quite a few guys on the team who you can't stand or the fans are bad, all that can ruin your game.

But in Greenville, it was flawless. Everything was perfect. Great fans. Great teammates. Great manager. We were all doing well. That was one of those times where the team played as a team and not as individuals. It was contagious.

Everything I was absorbing from this team, I remembered and carried with me for the rest of my career. I carried all that the following year, but we didn't have the same team. There were some different players and some issues with some of the players. That kind of pushed me back a little.

But at the same time, I told myself, "You've got to keep focused. Focus, focus. You have a career. You can't be stuck here in Triple A. You've got to move forward. If people have issues, let them have their issues."

I got called up on September 15, 1992, after we won the Southern League playoffs. That year was the first time I ever felt like myself as a pro player. What had been wrong in the past? I didn't know, and I didn't care. I just wanted to continue to put up those types of numbers from then on.

It was Grady Little who told me that I was named Southern League MVP. He came and shook my hand and said, "Congratulations. You won the MVP award for the Southern League."

He also told me I'd been called up. Grady called me into his office—and I knew it. I was already smiling, because I knew it was something good.

I was so excited that I'm not sure what I said. I think it was just, "Unbelievable! Thank you!"

Then I called my dad right away.

"Dad, I got called up!"

He told my mom, "He got called up!"

Then all I could hear were the screams.

BELIEVE IT OR NOT, THE FIRST TIME I GOT CALLED UP was the first time I'd ever been to a Major League Baseball game. I had no idea what to expect. I'd seen it on TV, but it's not the same.

They called me up after Greenville's last game. I traveled from Chattanooga, where we won the league championship game. I drove from Chattanooga to Greenville, packed my stuff, and the next day, I flew to Cincinnati. The Braves were playing the Reds at Riverfront Stadium.

I flew into Cincinnati and took a cab from the airport, which is in Kentucky, to the stadium. I couldn't believe it when I was going across the bridge from Kentucky into Ohio and saw that big stadium sitting there next to the Ohio River. It was an awesome sight.

I took a cab to the ballpark, and I couldn't believe how big the stadium was. I had to ask around to find out where the players' entrance was. I finally got into the locker room, and I was overwhelmed.

The first player I saw in the clubhouse was David Justice. He was like, "Wow! Congratulations!" I went over and shook everyone's hands and introduced myself to the other players. Everyone was congratulating me. They'd all heard about my season at Greenville.

I took batting practice and was trying to show off, but it wasn't a good batting practice because I was trying to hit the ball out of the ballpark on every single swing. Those are the things I learned later. Don't try to impress people. They know why you're there. Of course, I still wanted to impress them.

When the game started, I was praying that I wouldn't have to get in the action!

Cameras all over the place. 30,000 people screaming. All the pitchers looked 6'5" or 6'6"! It was frightening and very intimidating. Thank God, I didn't get in that game!

I didn't get in during that series in Cincinnati. My first game was September 18 in Atlanta. Houston was killing us 12–3, so I guess Bobby Cox thought I couldn't make things any worse.

He put me in to pinch-hit for Damon Berryhill in the bottom of the eighth, and I was freaking out. I was in the bullpen. A lot of guys started clapping because they knew I was going to get my first at-bat. That was even more intimidating, walking in from the bullpen. I was afraid to look to the left and see the people clapping.

I doubled off Rob Murphy, a left-handed reliever, in my first at-bat in the big leagues. I can still see Steve Finley, the Astros' center fielder, fielding the ball.

I didn't get to play much, of course, but I did pretty well when I got a chance. I had six hits in 16 at-bats for a .375 average with two doubles and two RBIs.

I could have started 1993 in the big leagues, and I was disappointed that I didn't. But at the same time, it is what it is, and I had to go wherever they assigned me. Greg Olson and Berryhill were the catchers in Atlanta.

Bobby Cox came up to me in spring training and said, "Javy, you know what? You've been doing great for us, and we all know you're capable of playing in the big leagues, but Olson is our regular catcher here—Oly and Berryhill—and he's still got another year on his contract. We'd like you to experience playing Triple A for a little bit, and then we'll see you soon."

I said, "No problem."

I went down to Richmond, and I felt completely positive because of what Bobby had told me. The fact that he had told me that I could play in the big leagues just motivated me to keep doing what I'd been doing.

I went to Richmond with a good attitude, and I started the season really well. Grady was still there. I actually set a Richmond record for batting average by a catcher (.305), and that ranked seventh in the International League.

I played well, and I got called up again. This time I got called up August 17 because Olson got hurt.

I still didn't play much, but at least I got to start four games. Just like 1992, I got six hits in 16 at-bats for a .375 average. Too bad I couldn't keep up that pace for my entire career!

The biggest moment came on August 21 when I hit my first home run. It came at Wrigley Field off Cubs reliever Shawn Boskie in the eighth inning. I kept fouling off pitches against Boskie. I was looking for a really low pitch, and I got it and hit it out. Of course, the fans threw the ball back like they always do at Wrigley.

I had a big game—three hits, two RBIs—and we won 6–3, so I felt really great.

Everyone congratulated me—Bobby, Pat Corrales, everyone. I don't think my dad saw it on live TV, but I remember how happy he was when I told him on the phone.

My ex-wife got rid of both those balls—my first hit and my first home run—and a lot of trophies and other things. But it's just a ball, just stuff. It's on video.

That meltdown in Durham in 1991 was long past, but it was something I needed to clear my mind and charge the battery. There is a point where, as a human being, you just have to let it out somehow. It worked. I never had another meltdown like that in my career.

THE ROOKIE

THE 1991 SEASON WASN'T EXCITING FOR ME, IN SPITE OF WHAT was going on in Atlanta. That was the "Worst-to-First" year for the Braves. It was crazy. But I was down in Class A at Durham having a meltdown and worrying that I might get released. It was great that the Braves were doing so well, but my thoughts were on trying to keep my career going so that I could get to Atlanta one day.

When I went back to Puerto Rico after the minor league season and saw that World Series between the Braves and Minnesota on TV, I saw Vinny Castilla was there. I was surprised he'd been called up. When he first came to the Braves, he was this skinny guy. I never in a million years thought he was going to be a major league player.

He was skinny, but then he started hitting home runs like Jose Canseco, beginning in 1995 with 32 for Colorado. That skinny Mexican guy? Yep, he had 13 home runs his first year in the minors (1990 at Sumter and Greenville) and 14 in 1991 (Greenville and Richmond) before getting called up. Great hands, great arm. Complete player. He was on the postseason roster, and I was surprised when I saw him there on TV.

The following year was another miracle season. That was even more exciting because of the way we ended up in the World Series: by beating Pittsburgh in the National League Championship Series. This time, I was there on the bench. I made the roster. I got called up when Greg Olson got hurt, and that opened a spot for me to be on the team in the playoffs.

As soon as the regular season was over, they called me the following day and told me I was on the roster for the playoffs. There were a bunch of guys who got called up that year, but most of them were sent home.

Because Olson got hurt, Damon Berryhill was the starting catcher and Francisco Cabrera was the backup catcher. But since Cabrera could play other positions, they wanted to make sure they had a third catcher, so they put me on the roster. I had one at-bat against Pittsburgh. The Pirates were killing us 13–2 in Game 6, so they put me in to catch in the top of the eighth inning. I batted against Tim Wakefield in the bottom of the eighth and popped out to second base.

At that point, both teams had won three games, so it all came down to Game 7. The Braves beat Pittsburgh the year before to get to the World Series, so the Pirates felt it was their turn this time…and it looked like they were right.

Going to the bottom of the ninth, we were behind 2–0 and only had five hits. The Pirates were three outs away from the World Series and sending us home for the winter.

We were playing at Atlanta-Fulton County Stadium, and I was in the bullpen talking to Francisco Cabrera all during the game.

People don't realize that Cabrera told me, "I'm going to bring in the winning run," before he even got called into the game. We were talking in the bullpen in the seventh inning, because that's when Bobby Cox started making changes, using pinch-hitters. Cabrera knew he was going to get called to pinch-hit for the pitcher.

He told me, "Don't worry. I'm going to get that base hit to win this game. We're going to win this game."

Technically, I wasn't even a rookie yet. I was basically just there to occupy space in case of an emergency. I was like, "Whatever!" But an inning and a half later, it happened just like Cabrera said.

He was the last pinch-hitter. If the game went into extra innings, I would be the one called on to catch. So things were pretty tense.

Left-handed reliever Mike Stanton was sitting next to me, and I told him, "Francisco told me he's going to finish this game."

Third baseman Terry Pendleton led off with a double against Doug Drabek. Then the key for setting up the inning happened when David Justice hit a grounder to second that Jose Lind bobbled for an error. That put runners at first and third with no outs. Sid Bream walked to load the bases, and the Pirates pulled Drabek for Stan Belinda.

Ron Gant hit a line drive to deep left that Barry Bonds caught, and T.P. was able to tag and score, making it 2–1. Belinda walked Berryhill to load the bases again, but Brian Hunter pinch-hit for Rafael Belliard and popped out. We were down to our last hope—Cabrera, who pinch-hit for reliever Jeff Reardon.

Francisco really battled, and then he did what he had predicted—he singled to left, scoring Justice to tie the game, and Bream came chugging around third and slid home to barely beat Bonds' throw to the plate. Just like that, we won 3–2!

Everything was so crazy that it was like the world came crashing down all of a sudden. I don't remember who was right next to me as we were running from the bullpen to home plate. All I remember is I was running as hard as I could and telling the guy next to me, "He told me he was going to drive in the winning run! He told me!"

There was a lot more excitement that night than when we won the World Series in 1995. It was unbelievable, and I wasn't even playing. I was looking around, and people were crying. It was just unbelievable! All the noise!

I got there and jumped on the pile with everyone else. I was looking for Cabrera to hug him and tell him, "You told me! You told me!"

Just imagine that year for me. I started at Double A, where we had the best record in baseball and won the Southern League championship. I won the league MVP. Then I got called up to the major leagues and made the playoff roster, then beat Pittsburgh that way and went to the World Series!

How many players spend years in the big leagues and never get in the playoffs? I was very, very fortunate. That was a surprise year for me, a very exciting year.

I didn't play at all in the World Series. We played well in the Series against Toronto. We did everything we could. They just played better. I guess what happened in 1996 with Jim Leyritz hitting that home run for the Yankees happened this time with Ed Sprague. We won the first game 3–1, and we were leading the second game 4–3 going to the ninth. Sprague pinch-hit and hit a two-run homer to give them a 5–4 lead, and we just never recovered.

They won that game, and then we went to Toronto and they won the first two there to take a 3–1 lead. We won Game 5 to get it back to Atlanta, but the Blue Jays beat us 4–3 in Game 6 to take the Series.

Sprague's home run off Reardon was the key to the Series. We were winning in Atlanta and were only two outs from going up 2–0. He hit that home run to put us down, and that was it. After he hit that home run, the whole Series was down for us. Reardon had been pitching so well before that, really well. But that's all it took was one at-bat to swing the whole Series.

That's the beauty of baseball—and the ugliness if you're on the wrong side.

I was blown away, though. People asked me about the season, and I said, "I'm overwhelmed."

When I got back to Puerto Rico, all my family and friends congratulated me. We had a press conference in my hometown to talk to the media, to explain the year I had and why I had such a good season. It was a very exciting time.

A lot of people in Ponce were Braves fans, not only because they could see the games on TV, but also because I was there. I went to all the television and radio stations, and I went to a winter league baseball game where a lot of the media talked to me. It was a big deal that year.

I DON'T REMEMBER MUCH ABOUT THE 1993 SEASON except that I hit my first home run. I got called up in August but I still didn't play much. Berryhill was catching all the time because Olson was hurt again.

We won the division on the last day of the season by one game over the Giants and went to the playoffs. I remember when Mike Piazza went deep to center field to help the Dodgers beat the Giants on the last day of the season. That put us in the playoffs.

We won 104 games in the regular season, but we lost in the playoffs to Philadelphia in six games. They kicked our butt.

That playoff with Philly was terrible. The bottom line was, they played better baseball. They had great pitching and great hitters.

Their fans were unbelievable. When we were leaving the stadium in Philadelphia, I thought we weren't going to make it to the airport. People were throwing and breaking bottles against the bus, spitting on the bus. The bus was rocking back and forth from people pushing it.

And that was after we lost the game—imagine if we had won! They'd have bombed the bus if we had won.

During that off-season, the Braves told me that the catching job was pretty much mine for 1994. I played winter ball that year, and my team won the championship in Puerto Rico. It was an unbelievable team.

While I was there, I was living in my father-in-law's farmhouse, a place he had inherited from his aunt. It was a little house sitting in the middle of the mountains. No telephone, no nothing. I mean *nothing*.

It took me 35 minutes of driving up and down the mountains to get there. There were chickens and all kinds of animals. The water came from a tank he built on the top of the hill. Gravity pulled it down to the house. And it was cold water, so I had to heat it in a big bowl on a gas stove to get hot water every single day. Sometimes I'd cook on the stove, and sometimes I had to get three bricks and put wood underneath and cook burgers or hot dogs. I like to cook and still do occasionally.

I couldn't stand living up there. It would have been okay if it was just for a day or a weekend. But just to get to the ballpark, I had to make a 90-minute drive to San Juan and then come back after the game. By the time I got back, it was almost 1:00 in the morning, and that was going through really dark roads. It was scary, but I survived.

My team was going to go to Isla Margarita in Venezuela to play in the Caribbean Series. But I got a call from the Braves saying they needed me in Atlanta for pitching coach Leo Mazzone's early camp for pitchers and catchers.

I was looking forward to going to Margarita Island for the Caribbean Series. Instead, I flew to Atlanta to catch bullpen in cold weather underneath the stadium. Okay! But this was my career. In Venezuela, it would just have been a fantasy.

Instead of going to the Caribbean Series, I caught some of the pitchers I'd be catching during the upcoming season—Steve Avery, Kent Mercker, Mike Stanton, Tom Glavine, John Smoltz. I don't remember who else was there, but I was there catching almost every day until it was time to get ready for spring training.

Then I went back home, got my stuff ready, and a few days later, flew to Florida for spring training. And I'm glad I went to Leo's camp, because when I got to spring training, I had a better idea of how to catch the pitchers.

I had a pretty hard time in 1994, my first full year in the big leagues. I wanted to be the National League Rookie of the Year so badly. Expectations of me were so high. The media was talking about me, but unfortunately I proved them wrong.

I was very disappointed. I put up the same kind of numbers I did in Durham in 1991—.245, 13 home runs, and 35 RBIs in 277 at-bats. I made the Topps All-Rookie team, but that didn't mean anything to me.

My numbers weren't good enough for me. I wanted to have the same kind of numbers Mike Piazza had his rookie year in 1993. Piazza hit .318

with 35 home runs and 112 RBIs his rookie season and was a runaway winner as NL Rookie of the Year. I didn't expect to be as good as him, because he was a freak in my opinion—but I wanted to be close to it, with 20-something home runs, and hitting close to .300. Of course, the season was cut short August 11 after only 114 games because of the players' strike. I was very frustrated that year, and the strike only made it worse. Dodgers outfielder Raul Mondesi wound up being the NL Rookie of the Year. I got a couple of votes, but I was way back in 10th place.

My dad always said, "I want you to have better numbers than Piazza... be like Piazza." My dad was always putting that pressure on me. Even as a kid, he made comments that he didn't realize put a lot of expectations on me. He's always been like that. Sometimes he talks and doesn't think about what it means to me.

You want to please yourself and your family as much as you can. It's nice to make them happy.

My dad would constantly say things to me like, "What's wrong with you? What happened to you? Why do you swing at bad pitches?"

I'd say, "Dad, do you think I wanted to swing at bad pitches? I don't know. My mind just wasn't there."

"Well, you need to swing at good pitches," he'd say.

We talked once or twice a week. He was able to watch every game on TV, and he always had to tell me what I was doing wrong.

If he was like Chipper's dad Larry Jones, formerly an assistant coach at Stetson University in Florida, it would have been different. Chipper's dad was a coach. He knew about baseball and the swing. That's why when Chipper struggled, he went to his dad to straighten him out.

My dad couldn't do that for me, because his advice was just, "Swing at good pitches."

I'm like, "I know that!"

"Then why don't you swing at good pitches? Don't swing at the bad pitches."

"That's what I try to do! The pitches look good, and then they turn out to be bad pitches!"

To him, everything looked so easy, but when you're up there at the plate, it's a totally different story. He didn't realize that.

My dad played some baseball, but he didn't get to a very advanced level. And he never coached, except my rec team one year. But he had a lot of passion for the game. He loved baseball, and he was the reason why I became a baseball player.

He took me to practice all the time. Sometimes he had to leave work early so he could do that. He did everything he could to help me. He got me to every practice and to every game on time. Every weekend, I would play two games, and a lot of times, he'd miss the first game because he had to work. He'd always make sure he was at one game at least. I couldn't have asked for a more supportive father than him.

I felt all these expectations, and I told myself, "I have to get all that stuff out of my head. I can't think about that, or else I won't be able to play well."

But it didn't work out. I tried to separate my hitting from my defense, but I got really frustrated if I went 0-for-4 or struck out with the bases loaded. And that affected the way I called a game, the way I caught.

I had gotten frustrated before, but I never let it affect my catching like it did that year. In the past, I left my frustration in the dugout so that when I went out to catch, I was still focused on calling a good game. But in 1994, there were some times when I carried my frustration with me, and that's when Leo Mazzone got pissed. The pitchers got mad too.

I had passed balls, dropped balls, and called bad games. I was frustrated, the pitchers were frustrated, and Leo was frustrated.

I told myself, "Do something good." I sat down for a couple of games, and when I came back, I hit well and caught better. I learned. It was a year for me to learn a lot of things.

But offensively it was still pretty frustrating. I wanted to do so well that nothing was happening. I felt like I was going back to where I was at Durham, and that's exactly what happened.

I didn't have a meltdown like I did in Durham, but I did have days when I couldn't sleep. I was frustrated, and there were some tears. I was telling myself, "What's happened to me? How can I get out of this?"

I did catch a no-hitter in 1994—Kent Mercker on April 8 at Dodger Stadium. It was pretty exciting, because it was only my 10th start in the big leagues.

That was one of the few games where I separated hitting from catching that season. I had a bad game at the plate (0-for-3 with three strikeouts and a sacrifice fly), but I left that in the dugout when I went back out to catch. I wasn't aware I was catching a no-hitter until the sixth inning. That's when I looked up and noticed it—a no-hitter!

Wow! I thought. *But how are we going to do this when we have to face guys like Mike Piazza, Raul Mondesi, Eric Karros, and Tim Wallach?*

The Dodgers had a monster lineup. They had one of the better-hitting teams in the league. They had three Rookies of the Year in the lineup— Piazza (1993), Karros (1992), and Mondesi (1994).

I tried not to let it affect me until the last out. I know it's a big accomplishment to catch a no-hitter. It was the first no-hitter an Atlanta Brave ever pitched on the road and the first individual no-hitter by a Brave since Phil Niekro in 1973 (Mercker was involved in a combined no-hitter with two other pitchers in 1991).

The Braves even gave everybody on the team a watch. It says, "Kent Mercker No-Hitter" right across the top.

We were using a lot of changeups. Merker's change was great that night. His fastball was popping, and he kept his curveball low, in the dirt, striking out 10. He had control of all of his pitches that night. He wasn't afraid to throw any of his pitches, and he knew he wasn't going to leave anything in the middle. He knew he was going to bounce it or could make them chase a bad pitch.

Chan Ho Park made his debut that night in relief for the Dodgers—the first Korean-born major leaguer. I remember he came in and bowed to the umpire to start the ninth inning.

Whenever anyone asks him, "Who was the first major league batter you struck out?" he says, "Javy Lopez!" I'm in his personal record book!

The last out of the no-hitter was Karros. He hit a grounder back to Mercker. I ran out to the mound, and there were a lot of hugs from everybody. Mercker is a great guy, very funny, very likable. Everyone was happy for him. Of course, I tell people the reason he pitched a no-hitter was because of the great catching.

If the pitcher has a catcher he doesn't have confidence in, it makes it hard on the pitcher to throw the pitch he wants. That night I showed Mercker that he could bounce the ball in whenever he wanted. He knew he could bounce it up there, and I was going to block it. I blocked a lot of pitches that night, and he got 10 ground-ball outs. But, of course, his stuff was outstanding—really, really good.

I could have caught two no-hitters. The other could have been John Smoltz in San Diego in 1996.

Tony Gwynn hit a double with one out in the seventh inning. Klesko went up against the left-field wall, and the ball went into his glove...and then out of his glove. It was San Diego, so they gave Gwynn a hit.

That was the only hit Smoltz gave up in eight innings (one walk, 13 strikeouts). Because we were ahead 4–0 and it wasn't a no-hitter, Bobby took Smoltz out after the eighth and let Mark Wohlers pitch the ninth. Wohlers gave up one hit, so it was a two-hitter. But I bet if Smoltz had stayed in, it would have been a one-hitter—and it probably should have been a no-hitter. He had his best stuff that game.

BECAUSE OF THE STRIKE, WE ENDED OUR SEASON EARLY IN 1994. I needed to find a way to make some money because we weren't getting paid. I was a rookie, and I didn't have a big salary or big contract.

Paul Kinzer was able to find me a deal with Sam's Club where I signed about 10,000 baseball cards. It took me four months—10,000 is a lot of cards and a lot of autographs. I was signing cards while I was playing winter ball in Puerto Rico—before, during, and after games! Everywhere—in the airplane flying back and forth between Puerto Rico and Atlanta—until I got the last one signed.

I have no idea how they used them, but at least I was able to make some money while the strike was going. Kinzer was a friend who was into collectibles, and he arranged appearances for players and took a percentage. He was working with me and some really big names, like Pete Rose and Mickey Mantle. He worked with a lot of guys. Davey Concepcion in Venezuela, Ryan Klesko. I think I got right around $50,000 from Sam's Club to sign those cards.

Kinzer was a friend. He allowed me to stay in his house during the season. The first year was for free. Then I decided to rent the little house he had behind his main house. The Kinzers are a good family. He wasn't trying to take advantage of anyone. It was a win-win situation for both of us.

He's an agent now and had a problem with the Braves in December 2008 when he represented Rafael Furcal. The Braves thought they had Furcal signed, but he wound up with the Dodgers. Sometimes an agent has to do what the player wants to do. If Furcal doesn't want to sign with the

Braves, then his agent has to be sure he doesn't sign with the Braves. And that's what Kinzer did. He did his job.

Because I was already in the big leagues as a starting catcher, I had the opportunity to be a starting catcher in winter ball that year, too. It was me and Carlos Delgado, who just finished his rookie year with Toronto where he played more outfield than catcher. We split the catching for the San Juan Senators.

That was my last year of winter ball. I had a controversy with the manager in Puerto Rico. He put me on the bench for two games in a row. That was my seventh year in the league in Puerto Rico. After seven years, I thought I deserved to be the starter. He used Delgado for two straight games, and I was so mad that I took my stuff and left.

The manager—Luis "Torito" Melendez—stopped me and asked what was going on. This was on my third straight day on the bench. I had to travel an hour and a half to the ballpark.

I was playing winter ball for the love of the game. But if I wasn't playing, what was the point? I'd rather have been at home with my family. So I left. He definitely liked Delgado more behind the plate, and I can respect that. He was a tremendous hitter. But the bottom line was, he's more of an outfielder/first baseman. I don't remember who the first baseman was, but Melendez decided to use Delgado at catcher. I said, "You have another catcher now. I don't need to come here."

Anyway, I didn't go the next day. We talked some more, and he got me to come back. Then I got a chance to play more. The days I wasn't playing, he'd tell me the day before that Carlos would catch.

With San Juan, I think I was making $2,000 every 15 days for two and a half months. The most I made in Puerto Rico was my last two years when I made $5,000 every paycheck. Now I think they're only making $1,500 every check. In Mexico, they pay $20,000 every 15 days.

We were all paying attention to what was happening with the strike, listening to the news, calling our agent to get the latest.

At the end of February, believe it or not, I decided to train to play volleyball. I was training because I thought the strike was going to last another year. I didn't hear about any progress. There was no news. No one had an answer.

Actually, I started and trained a couple of times to make the Ponce volleyball team in 1995. If there was no baseball, I was going to play volleyball. I'd get paid to play, but I wouldn't consider it being a "pro volleyball player." But I was getting ready to play.

I'd have been paid maybe $100 a game, something like that. We'd have played other towns in Puerto Rico. Volleyball is big down there. It would have been televised. I watched my sister when she was playing volleyball. There was always a full house, about 3,000 fans per game.

The owner of the team, Ebi Martinez, really wanted me to play. Before I signed to play professional baseball, I used to play with them, and I was pretty decent. I'd gotten taller since then, and he definitely wanted me on the team—the Ponce Leones. His daughter played with my sister many years on the Ponce team.

Normally, when there was a match, the women would play first and then the men. A lot of times, I'd stay after my sister's match to watch the men. I played with a lot of the players, so I'd watch them play.

That off-season I lived with my in-laws. No more driving to the mountains! I had bought an apartment, but it wasn't ready yet. So while it was being built, I lived with my in-laws and then moved into the apartment after the 1995 season.

But I was pretty excited when the strike was finally over. I knew I was going to start playing baseball and making money.

Everyone was very happy to be playing baseball again when we all got to West Palm Beach in 1995. Spring training was short—about three weeks—but it was enough. That's the way it should be! The pitchers threw a little more than normal. Obviously, a lot of them had been getting ready on their own. Everybody was ready.

It had been a very long wait from the end of the 1994 season on August 11 until the strike was over and we finally got ready to start the season on April 26. I'd spent a lot of time thinking about what went wrong in my rookie year. I was ready to turn things around—and I did.

WORLD CHAMPS!

THE 1994 STRIKE FINALLY ENDED ON APRIL 2 AFTER 232 DAYS— and it seemed like it had lasted even longer than that. We came into spring training in 1995 knowing we hadn't performed the way we should have the previous season. We let the Expos get ahead of us early in the season, and when the strike hit, we were six games behind in the standings.

Since the season wasn't finished and there were no playoffs, there was no official division winner recognized. The Braves' streak of division titles was three at that time but eventually reached a record 14, because 1994 didn't count in the record books.

In 1995 we didn't let the Expos get a jump on us like they had the year before. We started strong, and they were behind us. We stayed on top of them and never let that go. The other teams in the division were all about the same quality, and they all finished under .500. We finished first by a big margin—21 games over the Mets and Phillies. The Marlins (22½ games back) and Expos (24) were right behind them.

I had a good year and batted .315, which they told me was the first time a Braves catcher had hit .300 or better since Joe Torre in 1966. That was the year the Braves moved to Atlanta, so it had been a while. I didn't hit a lot of triples in my career (19), but I had four that year, which proved to be my career high. It also was the most by a Braves catcher since Torre in 1964, when the team was in Milwaukee.

Another highlight was June 6 when I hit a home run and single in the same inning against the Cubs. You don't get to do that very often!

The Expos had a pretty good team, but they were not nearly as good as they had been in 1994, partly because some of their players came to us—like outfielder Marquis Grissom, who was obtained in a trade during spring training. He was a key player for the Expos, the leadoff hitter you didn't want to see on base. But he was on our side in 1995.

We committed ourselves to winning as many series as possible. We didn't expect to sweep everybody, just to win two out of three. That was our goal.

Bobby Cox didn't talk about that, but John Smoltz, David Justice, and Tom Glavine did. We had player meetings, and everybody brought their opinions and questions and some motivation for the team. We did that every time we had a bad series. Our goal was to not fall back because of one series.

The year before, we let that happen too much. If we had a bad series, we'd carry that into the next couple of series. And in the blink of an eye, the Expos were ahead of us. We wanted to make sure that didn't happen in 1995.

So if we had a bad series, instead of putting it off, we'd have a meeting and talk right away. That was a big part of our success that year. Everybody was on board, and we kept it up all season. The veterans—Smoltz, Glavine, Justice, Mark Lemke—all agreed to have the meetings. We wanted to stop the bleeding right away.

It wasn't the first time we had meetings like that, but in 1995 we had them more often. By doing that, we became closer to each other. The second half of the season, I think everybody knew 1995 could be the year, that we had the team that could win the World Series. We had everything you could ask for in a team. From defense to offense to speed—everything. There was no reason we couldn't win.

Once we hit the playoffs, Justice made it clear to us that it was our time. None of that Buffalo Bills stuff about getting to the Super Bowl consistently but not winning it. We didn't want to get to the playoffs every year and not win the World Series. Justice pretty much let us know that. He was a big motivator. I'd say he was the unofficial captain.

Anybody who came from another team had to go through Justice. There were a few new guys—some of them were call-ups and some were acquired in trades—and Justice always paid attention to what they did when they got there. If a new player went straight to his locker, Justice would go to him and say, "How are you? My name is Dave Justice. What's your name?"

If it was a new kid, he'd be nervous. He'd tell Justice his name, and Justice would say, "Welcome to the big leagues. As a new guy, you need to introduce yourself to everybody."

So he'd make the kid go to every single locker and meet everyone and shake hands. That's what you need to do when you're new to a team. That's the type of guy Justice was.

On the airplane, he'd make sure the rookies stayed in the front, the veterans in the back. He wanted to make sure the rookies did what they were supposed to do right away. He had noticed how every year the rookies would come in with more confidence, acting more like veterans. He wanted that to stop. He didn't like that.

I'm sure someone did the same thing to him when he first came to the big leagues. He wanted to continue that tradition, and he could see it falling apart a little each year. Eventually it did disappear, but it wasn't because Justice didn't try to maintain it. Now when rookies come up, they act like they've been big-leaguers for years. Nobody says anything about it. Unfortunately that's how it is right now.

But Justice got a lot of respect from the players, and he made sure the guys—especially the young guys—followed the rules.

As a catcher, I was really happy that we got Marquis Grissom. He was a catcher's nightmare when he was on base. He probably wasn't the fastest runner ever, but he knew how to steal a base. Other guys were faster, but he knew how to get the jump. A lot of times, he got such a great jump that I didn't even throw to second. There was no chance to get him. It wasn't worth it to try.

He was a tremendous teammate too. He was always in a good mood. He always motivated his teammates. He was always in the game. Some players would talk about things in their personal lives, but not Marquis. If you were going to talk to Marquis at the ballpark, it had to be about the game, about baseball.

He was always a hard worker. He told me one time, "It doesn't matter what you do off the field. You can party, you can do whatever the hell you want to do, but when it comes to this business, you want to be sure you're here early and that you work your ass off. Go out there and give 100 percent. Whatever happens off the field, you forget about it. Once you get here, you make sure you give everything you've got for the four or five hours you're here."

Everyone has their personal lives, and different things are going on, but he said, "Maybe I partied last night, and maybe I didn't. But you're never going to see me show up late, and you're never going to see me sitting around doing nothing."

He told me that, and I never forgot it. That's exactly the way he was every day. He definitely motivated a lot of guys.

When we got to August and September, we knew we were in. At that point, we weren't thinking about losing in the playoffs. At least that's how I felt. My mind was set on going all the way. The only time I wasn't thinking that way might have been when Justice said, "We're not going to be like the Buffalo Bills. We're going to prove that wrong."

I'd forgotten about the previous seasons. I was playing like this was the first time the Braves were in the playoffs. That's the state of mind I had.

Of course, it was a little fresh for me. I wasn't there in 1991. I was with the team in the playoffs in 1992 and 1993, but I wasn't in the majors most of those seasons. And of course, there were no playoffs in 1994. I was part of it this time, and I felt like I was going to make a difference. The good thing is that everyone was on the same page.

That was the first year of the Division Series. We started with Colorado in the Division Series and then Cincinnati in the NLCS. Even though we beat the Rockies in four games, it was one of the toughest series I played in during my career with the Braves. They could have swept us. We just constantly kept coming back and scoring the winning runs.

I remember one play that was the key to winning that series. We were winning 4–3 in the eighth inning of Game 1 at Colorado. The Rockies had runners at first and third with no outs. Andres Galarraga hit a hard ground ball, and Chipper Jones dove and caught it down the third-base line and threw to second for a force-out. If Chipper hadn't fielded that ball, Colorado would have been on the way to a big inning.

Instead of a big inning, the Rockies only scored one run and tied the game. But then we won it 5–4 when Chipper hit a home run in the top of the ninth.

It was still a fight after that, but winning that first game in Colorado was huge and was the key to the series.

In the NLCS we beat Cincinnati four straight, but the first game went 11 innings before we won 2–1. Then, the second game went 10 innings, and I hit a three-run homer in the 10th to help us win 6–2. We battled that game. Greg McMichael did a tremendous job pitching the ninth and got the win. He walked Bret Boone to start the inning, and Boone got to third with two outs on a sacrifice bunt and an infield grounder.

Mariano Duncan came up as a pinch-hitter with a chance to win the game. I wanted McMichael to throw everything in the dirt—his best pitch was his changeup. So, I had to be sure I blocked everything and not let anything past me. Duncan grounded out, and then we won it in the 10th.

Once we got those first two games, we were going back home, and we felt like it was going to be easy for us. Mentally, at least, I was relieved. We knew we still had to work to win it, but we were going to Atlanta, and we were all pumped up. At that point, we just knew there was no way the Rockies were going to beat us the way we were playing. We ended up sweeping Colorado.

Because we swept them, we had to wait a week for the World Series. We won the NLCS on October 14, and the Series didn't begin until October 21. Cleveland was playing Seattle in the ALCS, and they were a couple of games behind us too. The Indians wound up winning in six games.

I REMEMBER ONCE THE WORLD SERIES BEGAN, I was hiding either at the hotel or in my house. I wouldn't go out. I didn't want to see what was going on. I wanted to concentrate on the Series. I didn't even go out to eat. At the hotel, I ordered room service every day.

A part of me was kind of nervous. It was a big deal, especially since it was just my second full year in the big leagues. I didn't want to let anything distract me. I knew people were going nuts everywhere, so I tried to shut that out as much as possible.

I'm not sure how everyone else handled it. I think there were others like me. I know when we were on the road, we couldn't go outside.

In Atlanta, you're at your house, but even then, when you'd get to the stadium, the first thing you'd see in the clubhouse was the media. I'd talk to the media first and get that out of the way and then go back to the trainers' room and stay there as long as I could—until the media had to leave.

Then I'd get on my uniform and go out on the field to practice. I tried not to go out until it was time to start. Most of the time during the season, I'd go out earlier to talk and fool around a little but not during the World

Series, because reporters were everywhere. I'd only go out when it was time to start shagging balls in the outfield or take batting practice.

When practice was over, some reporters might grab me, but I'd try to talk fast and get back inside as soon as possible. I'd go back to the trainers' room, sit on one of those tables, close my eyes, and relax.

I had this superstition about taking a quick shower before games. I liked to feel clean when the game started. After practice, I relaxed and ate, maybe read the paper or magazines, listened to music, watched TV, and tried to pass time until about an hour before game time.

Then I started getting ready—put on the uniform, taped my wrists, got everything ready. I always taped my wrists. That's something I started doing when I saw Seattle Mariners great Edgar Martinez taping his wrists in winter ball. He was a hitting machine. I thought that might be the reason, so I started doing it too. I don't know why players don't do it today. It feels great, and it helps protect your wrists from injuries. I started doing it in the minors and kept doing it throughout my career.

A half hour before the game started, I would go out on the field. Sometimes I'd warm up in the outfield, and sometimes I'd just stay in the clubhouse.

Bobby Cox didn't like the fact that a lot of times I didn't go out to the bullpen to warm up the pitcher. I wanted to do it, but I had a hard time facing the fans—whether they were cheering for me or screaming at me. I always had a tough time with that, because every time I went out there, they all wanted autographs.

I knew myself, and I had a hard time saying no to the fans. But when I was trying to prepare myself for the game, I had to say no.

When I said no, that's when I heard bad comments—that Javy was a bad guy. And that would stay in my mind. I didn't want to be a bad guy.

I didn't want to think that people didn't like me because I didn't sign an autograph for them. That was a distraction for me. I had a very hard time with that. To prevent it, I preferred not go out to the bullpen and catch, because that way I could avoid telling people no. Instead, I just tried to prepare myself in the batting cage. Most starting catchers don't care about that. I didn't do it all the time either.

I don't think it was a problem with Greg Maddux, because if he wanted me out there, I'd have been there. At Yankee Stadium and places like that, I'd go to the bullpen to warm up the pitcher because I really didn't care about those fans because they were so nasty anyway. But especially at home and places where I knew I had a lot of fans and where the fans were closer to the bullpen, I had a hard time going to the bullpen to catch. I just hated to turn down the fans.

Bobby didn't know about that. The staff probably thought I was just lazy.

Pat Corrales would tell me, "Bobby wants you to go out there to catch the pitcher."

I said, "Okay," and then I'd never go.

I only had that problem with the Braves. I didn't have to face the fans that close when I went to the Orioles. I wasn't as popular there as I was in Atlanta because I was new.

Fans are very important to me. I'd see all my teammates going out to the right-field line and doing sprints, and I couldn't go out there. I wanted to go out there with them, but I couldn't, because I'd see kids reaching out and yelling, "Please sign! Please sign!" And for me it was hard to ignore them and hard to say no.

Instead, I tried to avoid going out there, and I just prepared myself inside the batting cage. Throwing, running, stretching. When I finally went out on the field, it was time for the game. Then if somebody asked for an autograph, I could say, "Sorry, it's game time. I can't do it during the game."

I've always had a great appreciation for the fans. They're the ones who pay the money to watch us play and cheer for us. They've always been important to me, and even today, they're the ones who keep my image alive.

I care a lot about what people think. You want to be likeable. You don't want to play in a place where people don't care about you. That's kind of the way I felt in Baltimore. You try to be the best person you can be and at the same time, you want to hear that from people—that you are a good person. I wanted my family to be proud of me.

Nobody ever knew about this. I never told anyone. I felt if I told someone, it would be a very poor excuse, and I felt bad because I thought I should be stretching with my teammates instead of in the batting cage by myself. I'd much rather have been with my teammates all the time.

I don't know if this bothered any of the players or coaches, but no one ever said anything to me if it did. Since I was the catcher, though, I don't think anyone thought much about it. As long as I went out there and gave my best, that's all they worried about.

I didn't start the first game of the 1995 World Series. Maddux was pitching, so Charlie O'Brien was the starting catcher. I'll get into the Maddux situation and all the theories about why I usually didn't catch him later.

It was disappointing not to be starting the first game of the World Series, especially at home in Atlanta in front of our fans. But I also was kind of glad I wasn't playing because it was so intense. It was a close game, and I didn't want to be the one who screwed it up. If I had started the game, I wouldn't have been like that. But sitting there watching it, I have to say I didn't want to get in the game when the time came.

I'm pretty sure Eddie Perez felt like that when he used to come into the game late for me to catch Mark Wohlers.

I did come in to catch Maddux the last two innings. We were ahead 3–1, and they got an unearned run in the ninth to make the final score 3–2. I remember I told Charlie O'Brien afterward, "Way to go, kid. I'll take care of you tomorrow."

I don't remember much about those last two innings, but I remember Game 2, because I hit that two-run home run in the sixth inning off Dennis Martinez to make it 4–2, and we won 4–3.

That game was an intense battle. Martinez was tough, even though it was late in his career. But he had really good stuff. He was like Maddux—every pitch moved. He had a cutter, a sinker, and he had his tricks to give the ball more break.

That home run came on one of those at-bats when I wasn't afraid to get hit by a pitch. I actually was hoping I'd get hit by a pitch, but I definitely didn't want to strike out. There were a couple of times I fouled off balls that were about a foot off the plate.

Justice was on third base with one out, and the score was 2–2. I wanted to get that run in. I felt that was my time, my opportunity, and I wanted to make that happen. The count was 1–2, and I was just trying to stay alive. The next pitch was way outside, but I hit it out of the park to center field. It probably was a ball, but I didn't want to take any chances.

I knew Rafael Belliard was behind me, so I knew I had to be a good bad-pitch hitter, because Martinez was not going to throw me anything good with a weaker hitter behind me and first base open.

It surprised me when the first two pitches were down the middle, and he was going after me. He didn't seem to care that Belliard was behind me, so I said, "Okay. Be ready."

Then after two strikes, I started fishing. He wasn't giving me anything then, but at the same time, I didn't think he wanted to walk me either. So if he was going to throw a bad pitch, it was still going to be something I could handle. I knew he didn't want to throw something in the dirt with a man at third base. He didn't want that run to score. He didn't want to throw a strike, but he didn't want to be wild either.

I knew it would be a pitch that was reachable. I was so into it, so focused. *Hit the ball—don't strike out!* I thought.

I was very selfish in that at-bat. I could have taken a walk. But I swung at some bad pitches because I wanted that RBI so bad. I wanted to be the hero that night. I knew, via that camera in center field, there were millions of people watching me—my dad and everyone back in Puerto Rico. I wanted to be the one to bring in that run. I was chasing everything.

My dad was probably sitting at home saying, "Get a good pitch!" It's a good thing I hit a home run or he would have said, "What the hell were you thinking?" Well, I did it for you, Dad. I did it for you.

From Martinez's standpoint, I hit a good pitch. But his mistake was not walking me. He could have walked me and tried to get Belliard to hit into a double play. But they decided to go after me. It was their mistake.

When I hit it, I never thought in a million years that it was going to be a home run. That's why I was running hard. I thought it would be at least a double and the run was going to score to give us the lead.

I was happy, and I was running as fast as I could. Then when I saw that ball go out, I said, "I didn't ask for *that* much, but I'll take it!"

That was the greatest feeling I'd ever had in a game. I'd hit a home run in the playoffs to win the game, but that's the first and only home run I ever hit in the World Series.

Everybody was fired up, and that's what you want—that one big hit. Until then, everybody was concerned. It was tense. Then, *boom*—a game-winning home run.

Justice was waiting for me at the plate. Everybody was going wild.

Obviously, that pumped me up even more to play defense and make sure the Indians didn't score.

In the eighth inning, Alejandro Pena was pitching for us, and Cleveland right fielder Manny Ramirez got a single with one out. Then I picked Ramirez off first to kind of snuff out their rally.

Cleveland third baseman Jim Thome was up, and when Pena threw the first pitch, I saw Ramirez way off first base with a big lead. Fred McGriff and I had this signal: I'd try to get his attention before I gave the sign, and then I'd run two fingers through the dirt. That meant I was ready to throw to first base. McGriff gave me a sign back that he got it. He tugged on his pants or something. I don't remember what it was that particular game.

I called a fastball inside on the left-handed Thome, so I knew it would be a bad pitch for him to hit, and chances were he'd take it.

That was my plan—hoping he'd take that pitch so I could fire the ball to first base. If I called a fastball away, it would have been much harder to throw the guy out at first base. Thome would have been in the middle of everything. But with a fastball inside, I had Thome out of my way.

Pena didn't know what I was doing. I just set up way inside to make him throw a ball. I set up so far inside that Pena couldn't throw a strike.

Freddie knew I was going to throw, and he covered right away. I threw as hard and as fast as I could. My adrenaline allowed me to be that quick and throw that hard. It was a perfect throw, and when I threw him out, I thought, *Wow! A home run and a pickoff!*

I was giving everything I had. There was no more. I actually won an ESPY Award from ESPN for that play—"Baseball Play of the Year." People congratulate me more for picking off Manny than for hitting the home run!

In the bottom of the eighth, the Indians brought in Julian Tavarez to pitch. I came up second that inning. There was one out and no one on base, and we were winning 4–3. It was my first at-bat since the home run, and Tavarez hit me with the first pitch. But I don't think it was intentional, because of the home run. Not in a one-run World Series game.

Tavarez had such a big sinker. He hit so many people in his career. He just couldn't control his sinker. I got hit by him three or four times over the years. I always wore my elbow pad when I faced him because he always hit me right around the same area.

Belliard hit into a double play after that, and then Wohlers got them out in the ninth, so we had a 2–0 lead going to Cleveland.

My dad wasn't in Atlanta. He was back in Puerto Rico at work. There was a big party at his house—all my family was back there. I'm sure they were all congratulating him when I hit the home run. It made him a hero! I called him the next morning. That night there was so much going on that I just listened to his voice message. I had so many voice messages after the game. It was crazy.

My mom and my sister Elaine were there, and after the game, they were as happy as could be. We went back to the hotel, the Marriott Marquis in Atlanta. I was staying in the hotel to be closer to them. My mom and sister went back to Puerto Rico the next day, and the team flew on to Cleveland.

The team got to the hotel, got some rest, and then later went to the ballpark for some practice. My aunt and my cousin, who live in Maryland, came to the games in Cleveland.

We didn't think we had the Indians beat, even though we were up 2–0 in the Series. They were a good team and put up a constant fight. Every single out was a fight. We knew what we were facing. They might have even had a better team than we did. We just played better baseball, that's all.

Their pitching was good too. They had Martinez, Orel Hershiser, Charles Nagy, Jose Mesa, and Ken Hill. They had an awesome team. They had Thome, Carlos Baerga, Albert Belle, Omar Vizquel, Eddie Murray, Tony Pena, Paul Sorrento, Sandy Alomar. They had four guys who hit 25 or more home runs that year, and Belle hit 50. They had speed, power, everything.

Everyone said Cleveland had a better team than we did.

They had Vizquel and Baerga at short and second. We had Belliard and Lemke. In the outfield, we had Marquis Grissom and Justice and either Luis Polonia or Ryan Klesko. They had Kenny Lofton, Belle, and Ramirez. They had a better hitting team. We had Chipper at third and McGriff at first. They had Murray and Thome.

We had good pitching, and we were more motivated. We got hot. We had the momentum, and that's what did it.

We lost Game 3 by the score of 7–6 in 11 innings. I was 0-for-5, but I didn't strike out. I hit the ball hard a couple of times.

There was a lot of controversy surrounding Game 4, because Bobby Cox decided to pitch Steve Avery in order to keep Maddux, Tom Glavine, and John Smoltz on regular rest. Avery wasn't the same dominant pitcher he had been in 1991, 1992, and 1993. He was only 7–13 with a 4.67 ERA that year, which is why a lot of people were so surprised that Bobby decided to pitch him.

But Avery pitched an unbelievable game, and we won 5–2. Bobby decided to use him, and Avery just shut everyone's mouths. He pitched a great game, especially under the circumstances. It was all Avery.

His stuff wasn't the same as it had been earlier in his career. He wasn't throwing in the high 90s anymore.

He was throwing around 89 miles per hour. His breaking ball was working, and his changeup was working. He knew his stuff wasn't as good as it used to be, so he made sure he mixed up his pitches and made sure his off-speed was good. If your off-speed stuff is good, the fastball looks faster. So if you've got a good changeup, your 89-mph fastball will look like 95 because the batter is expecting something slower.

Avery made his adjustments and did everything he could with what he had. We were concerned about how it would go, but at the same time, we said, "Let's play. We've got eight guys to back you up. Let's play that way. We're going to protect you."

Instead, he protected us! He pitched six innings against a really strong lineup and only gave up one run on three hits.

At the same time, I'll never forget the good relief we got from Pedro Borbon. We were ahead 5–1 going into the bottom of the ninth. Bobby brought in Wohlers, but he didn't have his good stuff. He gave up a leadoff home run to Ramirez and a double to Paul Sorrento, so Bobby brought in Borbon with no outs and the potential tying run on deck. Thome, Alomar, and Lofton were coming up!

Pedro came in like a bull, and I was pumped up just watching him, the way he was breathing when he came in, saying, "Let's go! Let's go!" He was hungry. He was pumped. He was so pumped!

He struck out Thome looking and Alomar swinging, and then Lofton lined out to right field to end the game. Just like that, Borbon had a big save in the only World Series game he ever appeared in. He only had six saves in his entire career. What a huge effort that was!

I was 2-for-5 with two doubles in that game—one in the fourth inning off Ken Hill, a tough pitcher who was their starter, and one off Alan Embree in the ninth to drive in a run and make it 5–1.

Winning that game put us one win away from the trophy. It was a good position to be in, but we didn't really feel comfortable. We knew nothing was for sure against the Indians.

Of course, we lost Game 5 in Cleveland 5–4 with Maddux pitching, so when we came back to Atlanta, we knew nothing had been decided even though we were still up 3–2.

After losing Game 5, there was nothing better than having the next day off. That might have killed their momentum. If we'd had to play the next day, it might have been a totally different story.

We just chilled out on the off day. We took some batting practice back in Atlanta. I didn't have any family in town. I was staying with Paul Kinzer. I went to his house and relaxed, then to the ballpark for practice, and then back home to relax.

The following day when I came back to the stadium, I wasn't thinking that it might be the last game or anything like that. I was just trying to concentrate and keep my mind as relaxed as possible and not let anything distract me.

There was a group of Native Americans protesting outside the stadium because of the Braves nickname and the tomahawk and everything. That was a distraction, but I just tuned it out. Everyone was talking about Justice's comment about the fans in Atlanta, how the Cleveland fans were more electric and louder than the Atlanta fans.

"They'll probably burn our houses down if we don't win," he said. "They're not behind us like the Cleveland fans, who were standing and cheering even when they were three runs down."

I can understand where he was coming from, but at the same time, the way Jacobs Field is designed, the fans are a lot closer and more on top of the players than they were in Atlanta. The old Atlanta-Fulton County Stadium was so wide open—the fans were further away from the players—so the noise wasn't as loud as it was in Cleveland. It was just the area and the way the stadiums were built. We had a lot of great fans in Atlanta, a great crowd, and a lot of support.

He compared the Atlanta fans in 1991—when the Braves went from worst to first—to 1995. I wasn't there in 1991, but I'm sure they were outstanding.

The bottom line is that I didn't let Justice's comment distract me. I don't think anyone was distracted by it. We were completely focused on the game and didn't think about anything else going on around us.

But I do think that comment probably pumped up Justice. Some people get pumped up from something like that. It worked for him!

For Glavine, it certainly wasn't a distraction at all. I warmed him up. At that point, I wasn't worried about not signing for the fans. No one was signing at that point, so it was easy to say no.

Glavine was the same as he always was—typical Tom Glavine, nothing different. He just went out there like it was a normal game. And he pitched the same game he always pitched. He always made the hitter reach for his pitch.

The Indians were anxious. They wanted to hit every pitch out of the ballpark. That worked in Glavine's favor. He got nine fly balls, seven ground balls, and eight strikeouts in eight innings, which was good for him.

There might have been a few pitches that were a little out of the zone that umpire Joe Brinkman gave to him. I was catching, and I made sure I got that five inches away, just in case the umpire called it—and he did. It worked out. It would have been stupid for me not to set up there if the umpire was giving us that corner.

During my career, I always tried to challenge the umpire, to see what kind of game he was going to call that particular day. You always try him out. You set up outside, the pitcher throws outside, and he calls a ball. Okay. You stay away again and call the same pitch. If he calls a ball again, okay. Until he calls three or four balls in a row, I'm going back there. If he calls the first one a ball and then the next pitch five inches outside a strike, then I'm like, "Okay!" He can call that pitch a strike.

In that particular game, the umpire was definitely giving that pitch five inches outside. I knew the umpire was calling it for us, so I'm pretty sure he was calling it for them, too. But their catcher, Tony Pena, wasn't setting up five inches outside, which was their problem. If he did, they'd have gotten more calls.

But I made sure I was out there. If someone hit a home run, they better hit it the opposite way. I wasn't going to let that hitter pull the ball.

Belle went the opposite way twice. If anyone could hit it out the opposite way, it was Belle or Ramirez. Thome didn't go the other way much, but he could kill it to center field. I just wanted to be sure Glavine didn't miss with that pitch to those guys. I'd much rather see those guys on base—with four balls—than see them hitting a home run.

In the second inning, Belle led off with a walk. Eddie Murray came to the plate—they always had someone dangerous coming up—and Belle tried to steal on the second pitch. I made a good throw to Mark Lemke covering second, and Belle was out. Then Glavine struck out Murray and Ramirez, so what could have been a potential rally was shut down fast.

Glavine was on fire. He was locked in. Nothing affected him. He was so relaxed and into it. You could tell by looking at his face. He was so comfortable that it made me feel relaxed too. The whole team was relaxed. He only gave up one hit—a leadoff single to Pena in the sixth inning.

We were being protected by Glavine. He was so confident. He walked Belle twice and Eddie Murray once. Those are the guys you don't want to hurt you.

The ball wasn't carrying that day. It was cold and windy. But in the sixth, Justice hit a home run to lead off the inning. When he hit that ball, it sounded so solid. I didn't even see the ball. I saw his reaction at home plate, and I knew he had hit it well because he threw the bat and kind of started walking. I thought, *Holy shit! He got it!*

I remember a guy in the stands had a sign that said, "Justice, I hope your bat is as big as your mouth!"

Maybe David saw that sign—because it was!

It was exciting on the bench, but we didn't want to get too excited. We were like, "Okay, that's it. Let's get them one, two, three."

That was our attitude. As soon as we all shook hands after the home run, you could see everyone refocus.

I led off the bottom of the eighth inning against Julian Tavarez. He was challenging me with a lot of sliders. I knew it was either a slider or sinker in. He was throwing the sinker way outside to make sure he didn't hit me, and I just kept fouling them off. It was a 12-pitch at-bat.

The wind was blowing in, and it was cold. When it's cold, the ball doesn't carry very much. But he threw me a slider on a full count, and I was able to hit the ball pretty hard. Any other day, the ball would have been gone.

I was already celebrating. I had my arm up as I was running to first base because I hit it so hard. But when I got close to first, I saw Belle on the warning track, and he caught it. Out!

One second I had my arm up, and then the next I had my head down. It was embarrassing. But I said, "Who cares now? Three more outs, and we win the World Series."

Glavine threw so many changeups that when he threw that 85-mph fastball, it looked like 100. He threw mainly changeups and fastballs away that night. A lot of backdoor curveballs and some fastballs in to keep them honest.

There aren't many pitchers in the big leagues who can throw four changeups in a row. Glavine threw two in a row, and the hitters would think, *There's no way he's going to throw another one.* But then he would. He had such great control with the changeup that I was comfortable enough calling as many in a row as I wanted. There aren't many pitchers who can throw you the same pitch—any kind of pitch—three times in a row. Four? No way. Five? Doesn't exist. But I was doing it with Glavine.

We said, "Show us you can hit that changeup."

His delivery is what made it so good. Plus, he could change speed with the changeup. He didn't always throw it at the same speed. It had movement too. It dropped a little. Every pitcher has a tiny difference when he throws the fastball or curveball or changeup. There's something as a hitter you notice sometimes. It might be hard to tell, but something. With Glavine, there was nothing. Changeup, fastball, curveball. Same thing. It made it hard on a hitter.

I always wondered why he was so tough to hit, and I got to find out when he was with the Mets. He tried to get me out by staying away most of the time. Then I'd look outside, and he'd come in. That's why hitters had a tough time against him. They tried to think too much against him. They guessed a lot.

He once threw me a changeup when I was looking for a changeup, and I hit a home run off him. It was only 10 inches off the plate, but I reached it with one hand and hit it out to center field.

He threw the perfect pitch, but because I knew what it was, what it does, the location, everything…I had to reach as far as I could, but I was able to catch it on the barrel. Once you hit it on the sweet spot of the bat, you don't need to swing that hard to hit it out. The bat will do the job for you. It was ridiculous that I hit it out. One hand. He wasn't happy!

Then I faced him a few more times, and I started seeing a lot more in and out, more in. He got me the first at-bat, and then I got a base hit the next time. He made his adjustment, and I made mine.

As a catcher, that's what I tried to tell pitchers. Hopefully they understood why I called certain things the way I did. Nothing works all the time, of course, just like it wouldn't work all the time if the pitcher was calling his own pitches. Otherwise, every time I called a pitch, no one was going to hit it. There would be no hitting in baseball!

When Wohlers came in for the ninth inning of Game 6, I was really focused on getting the first out. I knew if we got the first guy, we'd be home free. That had been hard for Wohlers at times that year. But once he got the first one, he was automatic.

Lofton led off, and he hit a pop-up down the left-field line that Belliard ran down and caught, barely in foul territory. It was a great play. After that, Sorrento batted for Vizquel. He flied out to center, and Baerga did the same thing for the last out.

When Baerga hit the ball, I thought it might be in the gap. But Grissom got an unbelievable jump. Before Baerga even swung, it seemed like Grissom was moving that way. I was looking at the ball, and it looked like it might be in the gap. But when I looked down, Marquis was right there. He was effortless. He made it look easy.

Once he caught that ball, it was a totally different feeling than I had expected. When I was running toward Wohlers and jumping on top of him, in my mind, there was a rewind of the entire season, everything we had done to get where we were. All those moments were going through my head, and the more they were spinning, the more excited I was getting.

There was a big pile. I jumped on Wohlers, and everybody else followed. I thought Wohlers might jump on me, but when I saw he wasn't going to jump, I jumped on him instead. Everybody was on top of me, and I couldn't see. All I was doing was screaming, "Yeah!"

I could still breathe—barely. Somebody stepped on my head and knocked my helmet off. I was afraid someone else would step on my head after that. They were passing out the World Series champions T-shirts and telling us to put them on, and we were running around chasing each other and hugging and thanking the fans—just living the dream and enjoying it to the end.

The clubhouse was unbelievable. I was 24 years old and never drank so much in my life! Rather than spraying the champagne, I was drinking it. I had the biggest headache the following day. I sprayed a lot, but I drank more!

There was so much going on. All the families were in there. I spent most of the time with Pedro Borbon. We couldn't believe that just a couple of years earlier, we were in the minor leagues. And now here we were, celebrating the World Series championship.

He was with me in Greenville when we won the Southern League championship in 1992, so we said, "We're the good-luck charms!" He and I played together in Burlington, Iowa, Durham, Greenville, and Richmond. Four years. Then when I got called up in 1992 and 1993 a little, he got called up a little too.

In 1994 he made the team. In 1995 he was tough, especially against lefties. I hate that he blew out his arm. It hurt me. He and I had chemistry. When he pitched, I knew where to set up, what to call. He was nasty.

I think it was in Colorado the next year when he was throwing and started feeling some pain. But he didn't say anything. Instead of stopping and getting it treated, he tried to throw even harder. Then he threw a pitch, and it blew. He called trainer Jeff Porter, who we called Bubba, and his elbow was all swollen. I couldn't believe it. He still wanted to pitch.

We keep in touch. He's working with an agent—the Hendricks brothers, Randy and Alan—and represents quite a few players. And we'll always cherish the memory of the night we won the World Series.

LOOSEY GOOSEY!

AFTER THE 1995 WORLD SERIES, I STAYED IN ATLANTA FOR A couple more weeks to settle down. Then I flew to Puerto Rico. The day after I arrived, they had a parade, and all my family was there—the whole town of Ponce was there!

We did a lap around the whole city of Ponce and ended up in a place called La Guancha, where everybody gathered for music and food. It was a party—a big party!

I was in the back of this pickup truck with these *pleneros*. Pleneros are people who play the traditional music from Ponce. It's Puerto Rican music, but this type of music was born in Ponce. I felt like Michael Jackson that day!

I got to La Guancha, they were playing music, and there was a host who presented me to all the people. There were thousands of people. I did a little speech, telling everybody how happy and grateful I was, not only for being there but for the way they were welcoming me.

After it was finished, my family and I went to a restaurant. As a matter of fact, it was the restaurant owned by the guy who wanted me to play for his volleyball team: Ebi Martinez.

My wife at the time was pregnant with our first child. We had just won the World Series, my wife was pregnant with Javy, and then this party. The whole celebration was on November 4, and my birthday is November 5. So we celebrated that, too!

After the party and dinner with my family at the restaurant, we went back home. The following morning, my wife was having contractions, and Javy was born November 6, the day after my birthday.

A few weeks after that, Paul Kinzer called and said he had some signings lined up for me. There was a point when I was flying from Puerto Rico to Atlanta almost every weekend for these signings. And I got from

$3,000 to $5,000 for every signing. At the end of the year, it added up to a lot of money.

One of the signings was in a mall in Nashville. It was Ryan Klesko and me. We did a lot of the signings together. I remember we stayed at the Opryland Hotel. I had no idea about country music, no idea about Opryland or anything. I got there, and I was wearing tennis shoes and jeans. That night they took us to the Opryland show.

The host was Porter Wagoner. We went to his office and got to meet him. He was dressed like Elvis Presley. It was all sparkles everywhere. I wondered, *Who the heck is this guy? Is he a singer? Who is he?*

Paul told me who these people were and that Wagoner was the host of the show. Then we also met another famous country guy—Little Jimmy Dickens—an older guy in his seventies. He was in the Country Music Hall of Fame, but what impressed me was his wife. She was beautiful—tall, in her forties. We hung around there for a while, and then we went backstage.

Before the show, Porter Wagoner, who later got into the Country Music Hall of Fame, called me and Klesko out in front of thousands of people. I was like, "Holy shit!"

We were saying to each other, "You go first! You go first!"

They introduced us, and everybody was clapping. We'd just won the World Series! Everybody went nuts. It was like they were all Braves fans.

I took a bunch of pictures of the musicians who played that night, and to this day, I still don't have any idea who they were. Thank God we didn't have to say anything. We just waved and said, "Thank you very much!"

The next weekend it was Gulfport, Mississippi. That one was a mess, because I signed for two hours, but after two hours, the line was even longer. They escorted me out, and the people in line were mad. Some people ripped up my picture. What was I supposed to do? I would have stayed and signed if they would have let me. The people holding the show wouldn't let me sign for free. And I guess they didn't want to pay me more. I think I was paid $5,000.

I said, "That's stupid." If they would charge all those other people money, that's a lot of money.

So, when I went to Little Rock, Arkansas, that's what happened. After two hours, there were still more people. And I didn't leave until I signed the last autograph. I signed for almost four hours, and I made almost $10,000.

Ever since that incident in Gulfport, Kinzer told the organizers, "He'll sign until the last person, but it costs extra." And everybody agreed.

It seemed Tomahawk Fever was running out of control at that time—and it was a lot of fun. There were buildings where they only left on the lights that formed a tomahawk. There were billboards with our pictures in different cities and places. Braves here, Braves there, Braves everywhere.

There were pictures of me on billboards in different places. It was fun to see myself on billboards. Looking back, I should have taken pictures of them. Now the season starts and the only billboard you see is next to the stadium. Before, you'd see billboards with Braves miles and miles from the stadium. Of course, a lot of that was because of the Braves being on TBS.

In the 1990s, when the Braves were at their peak of popularity, girls wrote me a lot of letters with their pictures and phone numbers. They sent them to the Braves, and I got them in the clubhouse.

At the beginning, I started signing fan mail. But it got to the point where there were thousands of letters. I couldn't keep up with it. I signed as much as I could.

Unfortunately, among all the letters, there were some from card dealers who wanted me to sign cards so they could sell them. They didn't say that, but I could tell. They'd send three or five cards at a time.

It's too bad, but that affected the kids who sent me a nice letter with a card that they wanted to keep and collect. They were all mixed in together. Anyway, there were thousands and thousands of letters.

I hired a company that took care of my fan mail for a while. They had two ladies read every single letter. All I had to do was give them five autographs, and they had a machine that copied my signature exactly. They read every letter, and if there was something special they needed, they let me know.

All I had to do was go to their office once a month and maybe personalize some cards or do something extra. It wasn't much. They took care of my fan mail for a couple of years, and then it was too much work for them. They couldn't keep up with it. They were taking care of me and Tom Glavine. Between the two of us, it was too much for them, so they stopped doing it.

A lot of times, it was girls writing to me, so it was hard to take the letters home where Analy would read them. She didn't like it, but what could I do? It wasn't my fault. It created issues. So to avoid that, I just left them in my locker.

Everywhere I went back then, people recognized me and cheered for me. It seemed like 75 percent of them were female. It was an enjoyable time.

I mean, it's hard to have a following like that at the same time when you also have Chipper Jones, David Justice, Glavine, and Greg Maddux on the same team. But for some reason, a lot of fans liked to cheer for me.

I thought, *What have I done here? I'm just a catcher from Puerto Rico, and I don't have the numbers a lot of other guys have.*

Why? I guess they liked my butt! At least the women did, because the men were saying, "My wife loves your butt. Can I take a picture of your butt for my wife?" Some of them actually did that! Since I was the catcher, I was the only one who had my back to the fans all game. Maybe that was it! Some of the women put some unbelievable things in their letters. The one who went the furthest sent an envelope to our clubhouse in Philadelphia, and it had her credit card in it. I don't remember exactly what the letter said, but basically she wanted me to give her my sperm! She knew I was married. I don't think she was asking to sleep with me. She just wanted to have a baby that looked like me, so I guess she wanted me to call her to talk about how we could do that. It said, "Charge me whatever you want on this credit card as long as I get your sperm."

She gave the letter to someone, who took it to the security guard, who brought it to me. I opened it and saw the credit card. I had to show it to people in the clubhouse, and they were cracking up.

When I read it and saw that credit card, I took it back to the security guard who had brought it to me and told him, "Take this back to the girl that brought it." I don't know if they were able to find her or not, but he said they'd get it back to her.

Other women said they wanted me to marry them. Parents wanted me to go out with their daughters.

When I was younger and first came up to the big leagues, I had no idea I would be that popular or that anything like that would happen. I never looked at myself that way.

Analy was my first girlfriend in Puerto Rico—and my last. I never dated anyone else. Never in my life did I think I would be that popular.

The fact that I was an up-and-coming prospect was part of it, I'm sure. Then I played well, and we won the World Series. People started looking at me differently. I was part of the best team ever in Atlanta.

It's like you're living in a fantasy because you're on top of the world. Everywhere you go, people treat you well. Everything was free. I'd go to a restaurant, and they'd say "Don't worry. That guy over there will take care of that." Or, "Don't worry, the manager will take care of that."

I said, "Wait a minute. It should work the other way! In the minor leagues, when I didn't have any money, was when I should have gotten food for free! Now that I've got money to pay for it, it doesn't need to be free!"

I got great deals on cars. As long as I would drive their car with their tag on the back, dealers me gave a good deal. Everything was a deal in the 1990s. One year I drove a Corvette. One year I drove a Camaro. One year I drove a Mazda 626. One year an Audi. All free! When I could afford a car is when I got it for free! It was crazy.

Kinzer eventually became an agent and wanted to represent me, but I always saw him as a friend. I didn't want to see him as my agent. He said he could have done a better job for me, and he could have. Chuck Berry, my agent, is a very nice person, but looking back at my career, I made the least among all the top catchers at the time.

In my opinion, based on my numbers, only two catchers at that time should have made more money than me—Piazza and Ivan Rodriguez. But when I saw all these other catchers making more money than me I was like, "Are you kidding me?"

I played longer than them, so I made more over my career but not in the years when we played at the same time.

One time I did an appearance in Tifton, Georgia, a smaller town. It was scary, because I flew to Atlanta, and then Kinzer took me to this small airport. We got in one of those little airplanes. It was just the pilot, Klesko, Paul, and me. The runway was really tiny, and when that thing took off, it was like dancing in the air. Up and down...up and down...

Well, I pretty much had my head in Klesko's lap. I didn't get sick, but it was scary. But we made it! I'd been on a small plane before but never one that was going up and down like that one. Klesko? He didn't care. He's one of those guys who doesn't have any fear.

IT WAS A REALLY BUSY OFF-SEASON BUT FUN AND EXCITING.
When things finally settled down, we went to spring training in 1996 a little bit stuck up. You know, "We're famous now. We're the world champions."

All eyes were on us. There were a lot more people in the stands, a lot more media watching us. We felt more important, I guess. It was a special spring training. Of course, I always had fun at spring training. The difference was the amount of people watching. I don't think the Braves ever looked good in spring training, but when the season started, we were ready for the real games.

We had a tremendous team, just like in 1995. That's when Andruw Jones came up for the first time, and that created some stories—about Andruw and Justice.

I mentioned before how Justice wanted every rookie to act like a rookie. Well, Andruw wasn't acting like a rookie. Justice couldn't put up with that. To this day, Andruw has still never listened to what Justice said. Andruw is Andruw.

There was one incident when Andruw came up in August. He was a rookie, only 19 years old, but he had been tearing it up in the minor leagues. We had a lot of Latin guys—and some like Rafael Belliard, Eddie Perez, and I were veterans with a few years in the big leagues.

We were sitting in the back of the plane, and Andruw wanted to be in the back or close to the back. Anyway, he was sitting just in front of us. Terry Pendleton walked in, and he couldn't find a seat. When you see a veteran like Terry, you have to stand up. Well, Justice told Andruw he needed to get up and let Terry sit in his seat. Andruw was a rookie and needed to sit in the front.

I guess Andruw didn't listen, and he didn't get up. I think he thought they were playing a game with him, but Justice was serious. He didn't get up. Somebody else, a veteran, eventually got up so Pendleton could sit down.

After that happened, Justice put Andruw on the shit list. When we got to the hotel in Miami, Justice took Andruw's luggage to his room. Andruw was looking for his luggage and couldn't find it. He knew Justice had taken it from him.

Andruw waited until Justice was out of his room, and then he talked to housekeeping. I don't know how he got housekeeping to open the door for him, but whatever he did, they opened Justice's room for him, and Andruw got his bag.

When Justice found out someone took that luggage out of his room, he was mad. Justice talked to Andruw. I don't know what was said or what happened after that. I guess they got along. I really don't know.

Justice wanted to maintain some tradition, and Andruw was the first guy who started breaking up that tradition. Andruw was a tough cookie.

It was a couple of years after that in July 1998 when Bobby Cox took him out in the middle of an inning for not hustling.

Andruw always caught the ball differently, like a basket catch, and Bobby didn't like that. But he was catching everything and was the best center fielder in the league, so Bobby let him do it. But Bobby was waiting for his chance to make a point.

Then Andruw made Tom Glavine mad when he didn't hustle after that ball. Glavine screamed. Bobby heard it and took him out in the middle of the game.

Did Andruw change after that? No! Andruw never changed. He kept playing the same way. That was his style, like it or not.

I can understand Glavine screaming because Andruw didn't catch that ball. But at the same time, if he looks back, how many catches did Andruw make to prevent a double or triple or even a home run sometimes?

Glavine shouldn't have screamed—especially not that loudly. I can understand being disappointed in him on that play, but at the same time, he should have been grateful for all the runs he saved.

In 1996 Andruw came up and Pedro Borbon and Justice got hurt. I remember Justice took this swing when he looked like he was trying to be Fred McGriff with a big follow-through. He dislocated his shoulder, completely separated it, and he was out for the rest of the year. That was May 15, and it wound up being his last at-bat with the Braves because he was traded to Cleveland the next spring. He was a big part of the team.

To me, he was so valuable. When they traded him, the team wasn't the same. As his teammate, I always looked at him as the leader of the team. He had his things off the field, but what he brought to the field is all that mattered.

He was very disappointed about leaving the Braves. He didn't want to leave. He said general manager John Schuerholz told him he wouldn't be traded, and then he did it a week later.

In 1996 we had a pretty similar season to 1995. Our record wasn't quite as good percentage-wise (.593 compared to .625), but it was still very good. The main thing was, we still had the same chemistry on the team. I caught 135 games, which was an Atlanta record until Brian McCann broke it in 2008.

Going into the playoffs, we looked pretty strong, and we had a lot of confidence. We were pretty pumped up. It was in our heads to win the World Series in back-to-back years.

We swept the Dodgers in the Division Series. That was the year I hit a home run in the 10th inning to beat the Dodgers 2–1 in the first game of that series. I hit it off Antonio Osuna. Then after sweeping the Dodgers in three straight games, we had to face the Cardinals in the NLCS. We won the first game, but then we lost the next three. We were really in the hole.

I remember after we lost the third game, someone said, "You know what? Rather than being disappointed and worrying about only having one more game, let's have fun."

I don't know if I should say this or not because it's not going to sound good, but Borbon said, "Maybe tomorrow will be the last game,"—meaning the end of the season—"so let's get drunk!" And everybody looked at each other and said, "Why not? Let's do it."

You can't let this game get to you. That's probably why we lost three in a row—because we were too tight. So that night, we got hammered in the hotel bar in St. Louis. Thank God Bobby Cox wasn't around. The whole team was not there, but quite a few players were. We were all saying that we weren't winning because we were so uptight. It was just another day. That was our attitude. I was ignorant, but we were trying to do something to change the momentum.

The first two days in St. Louis, we were going to sleep early, getting our rest, getting ready for the game, and we lost both games. After two days of that, we were like, "Nah! We're going to get drunk this time." We drank all night. It was 1:00 or 2:00 in the morning when I got back to the room. I went to sleep and slept until 10:00 AM, and then we went to the ballpark nice and relaxed. Loosey goosey, though maybe some were a little hungover too.

And for some reason, my bat exploded! We had an 11–0 lead in the fifth inning, and I said, "We're going to win this game, and if we win this game, we're going to win the series." We won 14–0 with Smoltz pitching, and I had four hits, including a home run and two doubles.

We were going back to Atlanta with Glavine and Maddux pitching. After that night, I was so loose and relaxed, so confident, both catching and at the plate. It was like a switch had been thrown.

We beat the Cardinals three in a row by a combined score of 32–1 in Games 5, 6, and 7. It was insane the way we beat them.

I kept talking to Borbon and said, "Remember, Pedro, when we lost the second game in St. Louis and you said, 'Let's get drunk'? Look how everything turned out."

We killed them 15–0 in Game 7 to go to the World Series.

Just goes to show that sometimes you have to do things differently.

That's not to say that kids should go out and try our approach. It just happened to work for us that season. We just needed something at that point to change our attitude for the next game. We needed to be relaxed and loose. If that was going to be our last day together, we wanted to celebrate it. We had a really good season, won a lot of games, and made it to the playoffs. If that was the end, we wanted to celebrate.

I think I was more selective in that series. I actually was hitting well even before those last three games. My average was .417 through the first four games, but then I really got hot the last three games.

For some reason, I finally drew an imaginary red square in my head of where the ball needed to go in order for me to swing. That was in my head the whole series. If the ball was not in that imaginary square, I didn't swing. I tried to do the same thing in the World Series, and it didn't work. If you don't get the pitches there, it doesn't work.

But that particular series against St. Louis, it worked perfectly. Any ball around that imaginary square, I was hacking—and hacking hard. And I was taking my walks. My goal was to get on base—period.

In Game 7 I had two hits—my fifth double of the series that set an NLCS record and my third home run—and drove in three runs to give me six RBIs for the series. I batted .542 (13-for-24). The 13 hits tied an LCS record, and I was named MVP of the series. It was only the second time a catcher had won that award (St. Louis' Darrell Porter won in 1982). Mark Lemke (.444) and Chipper Jones (.440) also hit really well in that NLCS.

After the first game, I was just locked into that red square. During the season, I was so impatient. I was swinging at everything. For the first time, I concentrated more than any other time on trying to get pitches in that imaginary square.

So, a lot of times I took pitches I normally would have swung at. By taking those pitches, it became easier to take even more. I only walked 28 times during the season—I was swinging at everything. And I struck out 84 times, which was a lot for me. I was constantly swinging at bad pitches. So when we got to the playoffs, I told myself to be sure I got good pitches. I was locked in.

I was pumped up about the World Series against the Yankees. It was deja vu from the year before for the Braves. It was the same situation—big crowds, everything.

I never expected to be in the World Series to begin with, so to be there in back-to-back years was really amazing for me.

I don't read the newspapers, but when we won against the Dodgers in the Division Series, I watched the news and read the papers. It was fun to see all the good things they were saying about me. That kind of motivated me to make sure I didn't let down those people who were saying good things about me. I normally don't look at that stuff. Why did I that time? Too much time in the hotel, I guess. There was so much coverage—comparing the lineups between teams, all that stuff they do in the playoffs before a series starts.

After we won the NLCS, we celebrated like usual. We felt a lot more prepared for the World Series than we had in 1995. We felt like we had a complete team, even though we didn't have Justice, the kind of guy you feel even more comfortable with when he's in the lineup. But we were strong and completely confident going into the World Series. We knew the Yankees were a good team, but we knew the Yankees weren't better than the Indians were the year before. We beat the Indians in 1995, so we felt we could take the Yankees in 1996.

We started the World Series strong, winning the first two games at Yankee Stadium 12–1 and 4–0. I was thinking, *It's going to be easy. We're going to have another ring.* But baseball's never easy. We learned the hard way.

We had blown out the Cardinals in three straight, and then we blew out the Yankees in the first two games. But in Game 3 we had to tip our caps to David Cone. He pitched a brilliant game against us in Atlanta. He was unhittable. He was tough, and we lost 5–2. I had a single in each of the first three games but nothing special.

They pitched Kenny Rogers in Game 4, and we felt there was no way we were going to lose. We were ahead 6–0 after five innings, and it was

6–3 after six. But then Jim Leyritz hit a three-run homer off Wohlers to tie it in the eighth. That was a crusher. We never recovered.

Steve Avery came in to pitch the 10th, and they got two runs to win 8–6. Avery got the first two guys out, but then things fell apart. A walk, an infield single, and an intentional walk loaded the bases, and then he walked Wade Boggs to force in a run.

Their pitching killed us in Games 5 and 6. Andy Pettitte beat us 1–0 in Game 5, and they finished us off 3–2 in Game 6. Maddux pitched, and I caught him. He threw great, but we couldn't do much against Jimmy Key, their starter, or their bullpen.

We could have won back-to-back World Series. If we'd have won Game 4, the Series would have been over. We wouldn't have lost another game. But that home run by Leyritz…after that home run, the Yankees started a dynasty, winning four World Series in five years. That's where it began.

The key was us taking out Mike Bielecki in Game 4 after the seventh inning. They took me and him out in the eighth inning and put in Wohlers and Eddie Perez to catch him. He had struck out four in two innings…why take us out?

He came on in the sixth with the bases loaded and struck out the side— one, two, three. The next inning he struck out another one and got three quick outs. All he gave up in two innings was a walk. Why not at least start him in the eighth inning? I thought that was a mistake.

Wohlers would have been good for that last inning. That's what he was built for. Sometimes he was okay in the eighth if it was just to get one out—but not for three outs.

I was devastated about losing that game. I was so devastated, because I knew if we had won, we'd have been up 3–1 instead of tied 2–2. They swept three games from us in Atlanta. Our momentum was gone, and the rest is history.

Then we had to go back to New York and try to win Game 6 there. Their fan support was unbelievable. We did the best we could, but we couldn't get it done.

The Yankees had a bunch of old guys playing that year—Cecil Fielder, Darryl Strawberry, Wade Boggs was almost 40, Tim Raines was almost 40, Charlie Hayes, Mariano Duncan, Paul O'Neill, Leyritz. We were a bunch of young hitters against a team of veterans, and the old guys came out on top.

When we left Yankee Stadium, it wasn't as bad as leaving Philadelphia in 1993, but there was still a lot of booing and Yankees fans throwing stuff at us when we were walking to the bus. We got back to Atlanta and still had a nice welcome from the fans as we walked through the airport. It wasn't the same, but what could we do? That was it.

THE 1996 SEASON WAS PRETTY MUCH THE LAST TIME I SAW "BRAVES FEVER" IN ATLANTA. In 1997 it started going down, down, down. And every year after that, people started looking at the Braves as the Buffalo Bills of baseball, not being able to win the Series again.

We only won one World Series, but if you look at it, it's a lot harder to finish in first place 14 years in a row than it is to win the World Series in back-to-back years. Sure, the Yankees won four World Series in five years, but look at the history of baseball—how many times did a team go to the playoffs 14 years in a row? None.

It's a lot easier to win a seven-game series than it is to win a "series" of 162 games. And we won the "big series" all the time.

People still bring it up to me, and I give them the same answer: "Anybody can get hot at the right time."

Unfortunately, a lot of the times the team we played against happened to be hot at the right time. We were in the playoffs every year for 14 years, and most years we faced a different team. We were in the playoffs every year, and the team we'd be facing was in for the first time. Which team felt more motivated?

Some people say that the team that's been there before has an advantage because of experience, but it doesn't necessarily work that way. Some of the teams that beat us in the playoffs were the wild-card team. And they saw themselves as possibly not making the playoffs. Then all of a sudden, they were in the postseason.

Our motivation wasn't the same. We played hard and did everything we could to win. But unfortunately baseball is about whoever gets hot at the end. Anybody can win a series of seven games. Anybody. We weren't the hotter team at those particular moments, and that was it. I wish we could have won a lot more World Series, but it is what it is.

We'll take that 14-year run anytime, and a lot of players on other teams would take the same thing. A lot of managers would like to have that run by the Braves.

I was very, very fortunate to be involved in that run. A lot of guys play a long time and never get to the playoffs. I can't complain. From the first time I got to the big leagues, I was in the playoffs and often the World Series.

Not many players in baseball history can say that.

7

OCTOBER MISERY

IN 1997, I HIT .295. I WAS HITTING .298 GOING INTO THE FINAL WEEK but couldn't get up to .300. It would have been nice to hit .300.

I finally made the All-Star team that year. In 1995 I thought I was going to be selected, but I wasn't. They picked Mike Piazza and Darren Daulton. I was kind of bummed about it. Daulton was hitting .221 at the break, and I was hitting .274. I told the media I was disappointed, but I knew he was the veteran.

My first All-Star Game was 1997 with Piazza, Todd Hundley, and Charles Johnson. I was very excited. Everyone told me "it was about time," and in my mind, I should have made it a couple of times before that.

But I was happy to be there to back up Piazza. I got my first All-Star at-bat and happened to hit a home run. Someone from Cooperstown talked to me about sending the bat to the Hall of Fame, because I was just the 11th player to hit a home run in his first All-Star at-bat.

The game was played in Cleveland. The American League led 1–0 when I hit my home run in the top of the seventh to tie it. I hit it off Jose Rosado, a lefty with Kansas City who also was from Puerto Rico. But the American League scored two in the bottom of the inning and won 3–1. Rosado actually got credit for the win.

When I hit it, I knew it was gone—I just didn't know if it would be fair. It hit the pole! When I saw it hit the pole, it was a great feeling to run the bases and then have all these big guys—Jeff Bagwell, Barry Bonds, Tony Gwynn, Andres Galarraga, Chipper Jones—shaking my hand.

In the sixth, Ken Griffey Jr. had fouled off a pitch that fractured my hand—a hairline fracture in my thumb. They had to take me out after the seventh inning, and I had to go on the disabled list until July 22. That's when I started using the thumb guard. My thumb hurt like crazy. I caught that last batter, but every time the pitcher threw, I felt it. Of course, I didn't want to come out—it was the All-Star Game, after all.

After the game, there were a lot of reporters talking to me, including media from Puerto Rico. I'm sure my home run was a big deal for my dad back home, and the game was a big deal for Puerto Rico. I hit a home run, Sandy Alomar was the MVP, and Rosado was the winning pitcher. Three of the key people were from Puerto Rico. Roberto Alomar was in the game, and so was Edgar Martinez. Quite a few Puerto Ricans.

The following year, I made the team again. The game was in Colorado, and Roberto was the MVP. It was tough, a really tough All-Star Game.

I was in the Home Run Derby that year too. I hit five out. I was the second hitter, and I was very nervous. The whole nation was watching me hit. I thought, *Five, that's not too bad. Piazza didn't hit one in his first two years.*

That day, after the Home Run Derby, there was a big party for all the All-Stars. The next day, Piazza started the game at catcher, and I entered the game in the top of the sixth for him.

Ugueth Urbina from the Expos started that inning, and unfortunately, he didn't have his control that day. I tried to block every pitch the best I could. But he threw every pitch hard and against the ground. I couldn't block everything. Out of every five pitches, I was probably blocking three. The other two bounced away.

Then I'd call a fastball and he'd throw a slider. He was having a hard time seeing my signs. It was terrible.

Once they took him out, I was able to catch normally again. But the damage had been done. When he came in, we were leading 6–5. But the American League loaded the bases right away and scored the tying run on my passed ball. With two outs, Urbina threw a wild pitch, and another run scored, and they got a hit for another run. He gave up three runs, and the American League went ahead 8–6.

Maybe it didn't matter, because they beat us 13–8, but it was an inning from hell. It felt like it lasted forever. They kicked our butts, anyway.

I caught Jeff Shaw in the eighth and Robb Nen in the ninth. Urbina was the losing pitcher. I only got one at-bat, and I struck out in the seventh inning.

I heard some boos. I'm sure it was because of the trouble I had catching Urbina. He couldn't see my signs. He was throwing pitches I wasn't calling. Everything was in the dirt. I had to block, block, block. I had a passed ball. I'd be waiting for a slider…and he'd throw me a sinker.

Then I came up to bat, I wasn't exactly feeling good, and I had to face John Wetteland, who was nasty. Anyway, I tried not to be pissed because it was an All-Star Game. But my All-Star Game was ruined. I didn't have any fun at all! That inning and that at-bat ruined my All-Star Game. It was terrible.

I had another All-Star experience after the season that helped make up for it a little bit. I was on the team of Major League All-Stars that toured Japan. I played in five games and hit .375 and had a great time.

Going to Japan was a tremendous experience. Their stadiums are very impressive, and I liked how their fans were so supportive of the teams. The Japanese have a totally different style of playing. They're very hard workers. If we practiced four hours, they'd practice eight.

The pitchers don't throw anything straight. Every pitch is a sinker, a cutter, a knuckleball, every kind of breaking ball there is. Then every once in a while, they'd throw a fastball when we least expected it. They only throw it 80 miles per hour, but it seemed like 100 because they threw so much junk!

All their players were fast runners—the catchers, everybody could steal bases. Ichiro Suzuki was playing for them that year, because he hadn't come over here to start playing yet. He was a nightmare! He was running like crazy.

We were able to tour the Mizuno facilities, and I was even able to make my own bat on the lathe. That was the year Sammy Sosa hit 66 home runs and Mark McGwire hit 70. The Japanese loved Sammy. Everywhere he went, there was a mob of people. It was unbelievable.

I wasn't Sosa, but people still followed me everywhere I went. Everyone wanted autographs, but it was a tremendous experience. They treated everyone first-class. It was expensive, though. Rey Ordonez, Vinny Castilla, and I went out to dinner one night with our wives, and the bill was $1,500 for three couples. The Kobe beef was tremendous, though!

I didn't make the National League All-Star team again until 2003, when I was the starting catcher. The game was in Chicago at U.S. Cellular Field. I didn't have any hits, but I did have two good at-bats. I hit the ball hard both times, a grounder to third off Roger Clemens in the third inning and a fly ball to center in the fifth off Shigetoshi Hasegawa.

We were winning 5–1 when I left the game, and Paul Lo Duca came in for me in the bottom of the sixth inning. The American League ended up beating us 7–6, but it was a lot of fun. I really enjoyed that All-Star Game.

THE MARLINS FINISHED SECOND TO US IN 1997, but they won the wild card and kicked our butts in the NLCS after we swept three games from Houston in the Division Series. They had a tremendous pitching staff—Kevin Brown, Livan Hernandez, Al Leiter, and Robb Nen, among others—and played really well.

The umpire—Eric Gregg—really helped them in Game 5 too. Livan Hernandez was pitching. I guess Gregg wanted to get out of there. I don't know if he had something against us or what. It was ridiculous, and everyone knew it.

As a catcher, I was watching every single call on the TV monitor in the dugout. Florida's catcher, Charlie Johnson, was setting up way outside, and Gregg was giving them strikes. I was trying to do the same thing, but he wasn't calling them for us. There were quite a few times when I said to Gregg, "What's going on? Is it too outside? Okay…"

Then when I was at bat, he was calling pitches way outside. I said to him, "Isn't that the way we've been pitching, and you're calling them balls?"

He always had a lot of patience with players. He never got mad. He just said, "Oh, no, no! That's a ball. Oh, no, no, that's a strike." Like it was no big deal.

The way that game ended was perfect for the way Gregg called the whole game—he called out Fred McGriff on a ball that was two feet outside. It really was unbelievable.

Gregg knew he was in Miami and that nothing was going to happen to him. I don't think he would have called the same pitches in Atlanta, because he wouldn't have made it out of the parking lot. It was terrible.

After the game, there was no player who didn't talk about it to the media. We all felt the same way. It was so obvious. But, at the same time, it was just that one game.

The Marlins won that game 2–1. Our only run was a home run by Michael Tucker in the second inning, and we only had two other hits. Hernandez had 15 strikeouts, but I'd credit a lot of them to Gregg.

That gave Florida a 3–2 lead in the series. If we'd have won that game, who knows? But then they beat us 7–4 in Game 6 and went on to the World Series, where they beat Cleveland to become the first wild-card team to win the Series.

You have to give credit to the Marlins, because they played really good baseball. Their pitching was tough, and they just played better than we did. We didn't hit the way we should have. They had a good team—Edgar Renteria, Bobby Bonilla, Devon White, Gary Sheffield, Moises Alou, Jeff Conine, Charles Johnson. They had a darn good team.

But we outhit the Marlins .253 to .199 over the six-game series. We had a good team too. The series was 2–2, and then we lost the Eric Gregg game, and Kevin Brown beat Tom Glavine in Game 6. It was Game 5 that made the difference.

We always had good pitching, but that year it was especially good. Bill James, the stats expert, rated it the best pitching staff ever because the team ERA of 3.18 was 32 percent better than the league average. We led the league in most other statistical categories too—fewest hits, fewest runs, fewest home runs allowed, fewest walks.

We had Maddux, Glavine, Smoltz, and Denny Neagle in the starting rotation. Neagle won 20, Maddux 19, Smoltz 15, and Glavine 14. Wohlers was the closer and saved 33 games. That was also Kevin Millwood's rookie year.

As a catcher, what more can you ask for than a pitching staff like that? Not only was it fun to catch a staff like that, but it made my job so easy. It's hard for a catcher to catch a staff like that and then go to another team and catch "regular" pitchers.

Look at their ERAs. Maddux's was 2.20, and he finished second to Pedro Martinez for the Cy Young. Glavine 2.96. Neagle 2.97. Smoltz 3.02. It was sick!

And it was contagious. One guy pitched a good game, and the next one followed him, trying to do better. Then the next and the next. It was enjoyable to catch them. We had quick games, which was really good for me. It was fun.

The only thing I had trouble with was Glavine's move to home plate. It wasn't as quick as I'd have liked it to be, which meant runners stole bases. Smoltz was okay when he used the slide step. But other than that, catching those guys was heaven. Every catcher would kill to have a pitching staff like that.

Klesko led the team in home runs with 24, and I was next with 23. We didn't have one really big threat, but we had four guys with 21 or more.

We were all blown away when they traded Justice and Marquis Grissom to Cleveland for Kenny Lofton and Alan Embree on March 25. Everyone was surprised. Justice was saying good-bye to everyone, and you could tell he was about to cry. He didn't want to leave the Braves, but he had no choice.

If we were trading Grissom, and I didn't think we should, we definitely needed a leadoff hitter. And I would have tried to trade someone else, not Justice. Justice knew what it takes to win. He knew what it takes to bounce back from a slump. But trading Grissom *and* Justice?

Lofton just played that one year with us. He hit .333, fourth in the league, but his personality didn't fit in the organization. Don't get me wrong. He was a really cool guy, and we hung out together a few times. He tried to bring his own rules. Unfortunately, he was on Bobby's shit list. Back then, Bobby didn't want anyone to wear Oakley sunglasses. We had those old-style flip glasses, and those were the only glasses we were allowed to wear in 1997. Even though everyone had Oakleys, we had to follow the rules.

Lofton had his own Oakleys, and not only did he wear them, but he put them on the top of his cap. Everyone does that now, but Bobby didn't like it because he didn't want them to cover the *A* on the cap. Lofton talked Bobby out of it—or else Bobby just let him do it.

He did all kinds of stuff that Bobby didn't like. When he got a walk, he'd flip the bat instead of giving it to the batboy and walking to first base. He did things to try to get people's attention, and Bobby didn't like that.

He got along with the other players, but he was in his own world.

If you told someone you wanted to trade Grissom and Justice for Lofton and Embree and at the same time trade Jermaine Dye and Jamie Walker for Michael Tucker and Keith Lockhart from Kansas City, they would say, "Well, there must be more to it than that." I couldn't understand how that was a fair exchange for the Braves.

Grissom and Justice were leaders on the team. They were winners. And Dye was one of our top prospects. He had speed, the arm, the bat, and wound up being the World Series MVP for the White Sox in 2005.

Here I am on my bike outside my childhood home in Ponce, Puerto Rico.

This is a picture of our house in Ponce. I was lucky to grow up around so many good people and so many friends.

My family and I were very close growing up, and we still are. That's me sitting to my mother's right.

When I was nine years old, I tried out for the local team in Ponce, the Criollos. I am standing on the far right.

This was taken the day Jorge Posada signed me to my contract with the Atlanta Braves. My dad is in the background.

I am wearing the uniform of my first professional baseball team, the Metros, in Puerto Rico.

I was also proud to play for my hometown team, the Leones de Ponce.

I celebrated with teammates Rafael Belliard and David Justice after hitting a two-run, game-winning home run in Game 2 of the 1995 World Series.
(AP Images)

My friend and teammate, Pedro Borbon, got the save in Game 4 and put us one win away from a World Series championship.
(AP Images)

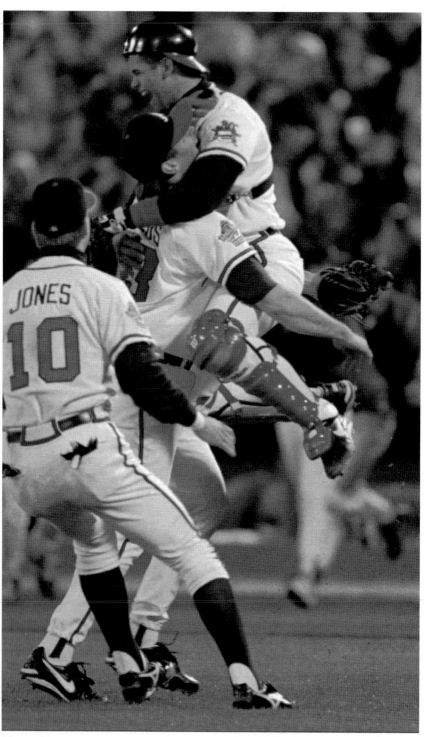

Victory! I jumped into Mark Wohlers' arms after we won Game 6 by a score of 1–0. (AP Images)

This is a picture of Ted Turner and me after I won the NLCS Most Valuable Player award in 1996. (AP Images)

I hit a home run in my very first All-Star Game at-bat in 1997 off Kansas City's Jose Rosado. (AP Images)

Bobby Cox managed me my entire Braves career. He retired in 2010 with 2,149 career wins with Atlanta. (AP Images)

My dad, Jacinto, my son, Javy Jr., and me. Family has always been the most important thing in my life.

Why they made those two trades right before the start of the 1997 season, I don't know. It didn't make any sense to me or to my teammates.

That's probably why Fred McGriff only hit 22 home runs that year. He didn't have Justice as protection behind him. He didn't see any good pitches with Justice gone. Maybe Justice was a little controversial, and general manager John Schuerholz didn't like that. But he wasn't hurting the team. He had his issues with his divorce and personal life, but who cares? That had nothing to do with the team and how he was playing. Nothing.

I wasn't too happy. The guy who did the best job for us out of all the players we got was Lockhart. He had tremendous hands that could replace Mark Lemke at second base. Anything around second base was an out. He could hit, had some power, produced in the clutch, and was a good teammate.

Tucker, Lofton, and Embree? None of them were around very long. Justice and Grissom wound up in the World Series again that year with Cleveland, and it seemed like Justice was in the World Series or at least the playoffs almost every year.

We'll never really know why they made those trades. Only Schuerholz and Bobby Cox know. But that was ridiculous. Lofton was a great leadoff hitter. He'd get on base, and he could steal. He did a great job for us, don't get me wrong. He hit .333 for us, and he stole 27 bases—but he also got caught a lot (20 times, 57.4 percent success rate).

When the Marlins knocked us out in the NLCS, I was starting to get sick of coming up short in the playoffs.

We had a great team and a great season, but then we lost. It's not a good feeling, because at that point, it didn't matter how good we had done in the season. When you lose like that in the playoffs, it makes the whole season feel like it was terrible. You don't look at the good side of it.

We cared about winning in the playoffs and making it to the World Series. If we lost in the World Series, at least we had made it to the end. When we fell short so many times, that's what made us feel sick.

A lot of people asked me, "Why is this happening?" and I couldn't answer them. It's something that was in our heads, because every time we made it to the playoffs, the media, fans, everyone wanted to talk about it. So when we got to the playoffs—*boom!* Automatically, we couldn't help but think about it. The story repeated itself.

Maybe we tried too hard, and trying too hard wouldn't allow us to play our game. We tried so hard because we wanted to prove the media and the fans wrong. The Las Vegas gamblers probably bet against us as soon as we made it, because they knew! We wanted to prove everyone wrong, and in trying to do that, we tried too hard. It's the only answer I can come up with.

Every time we went to the playoffs, the media was asking the same question to every player. "Is this going to be the year?"

We'd say, "We feel pretty good about it. We'll see."

That put it in our heads, and then we tried too hard.

Also in 1997 we moved into Turner Field and left Atlanta-Fulton County Stadium. That was a good experience. I liked Fulton County. I think it was beautiful. But Turner Field is too. I remember everyone was betting to see who would be the first one to hit a home run. It was Tucker. I had the first double.

Everybody was excited about moving into Turner Field. It was a good feeling, playing in a new stadium. More fans. Everything was different. There was a very nice clubhouse.

We also moved spring training from West Palm Beach to Disney World in Orlando. We played our last spring-training game of 1997 at Disney and then moved there full-time in 1998. It was very enjoyable to play there. I really liked West Palm Beach just because there was so much to do there. I used to fish a lot. Some of the other players had poles, and I'd go with them. We had those big empty paint cans, and we'd fill them up with fish. I don't know what they did with all of them. I never ate them, but it was fun catching them.

The field wasn't as pretty as Disney, and there weren't as many fans. Orlando is the best for that. I liked being at Disney World. My kids enjoyed it! All the theme parks in Orlando were great. It was nice for a week, but then I got a little tired of it.

That's why West Palm was better, in my opinion. I didn't get tired of seeing the ocean and I could do something different every day. Good golf courses there, too, though I didn't play back then.

WE PICKED UP ANDRES GALARRAGA AT FIRST BASE AND WALT WEISS AT SHORTSTOP, both via free agency, for the 1998 season. We had a pretty decent team and won 106 games. No Kenny Lofton. We had four guys with 30 or more home runs—Andruw Jones (31), Chipper (34), me (34), and Galarraga (44). I set the franchise record for home runs and RBIs by a catcher, breaking Joe Torre's records.

Our hitting was contagious, and it was fun. I think Galarraga was our inspiration. We hit for a high average (.272) and all those home runs (215) too. I set career highs at the time in home runs, RBIs (106), runs (73), and hits (139). From August 29 to September 1, I homered in four straight games. My ratio of a home run every 14.4 at-bats ranked sixth in the league.

I was very happy when we got Galarraga. He's such a great guy. We called him Big Cat. I knew him from talking with him during practice when he was with Colorado. Big Cat was big-time protection! Everyone felt the same way having Galarraga in there.

Unfortunately, he had cancer the following year and missed the entire season. That was awful for him and for everyone, but we found a way to win again—without him and without me too. I tore my ACL in the middle of the season.

But we had a tremendous season in 1998. We swept the Cubs in the Division Series. They had a pretty good team, obviously, because they made the playoffs.

We won the first game 7–1, but we were losing 1–0 in the bottom of the ninth inning of Game 2. Then I hit a one-out home run off Kevin Tapani to tie the game in the ninth, and we won 2–1 in the 10th.

Tapani was striking out guys with his slider away and getting a lot of ground balls with the sinker in. I made my adjustment that at-bat. I was a pretty good breaking-ball hitter. I was having a hard time hitting fastballs, especially sinkers. So I was looking for off-speed stuff and trying to stay back on it.

I'm sure their scouting report said, "Javy's a pretty good breaking-ball hitter." So they were throwing me fastballs. That ninth inning, after facing Tapani three times, I was looking for the fastball, the sinker in. I stayed a little bit off the plate, in case he threw me the same thing.

He tried to throw that sinker in again, to keep me off balance and try to jam me. But I was prepared to take a bigger hack at that pitch. I think it was a fastball, a sinker in, and I got hold of it. I remember choking the bat a little bit too. He was trying to get ahead the first couple of pitches, so I was ready to swing. I hit the second pitch out to left field. It's the best feeling in the world to hit a home run in a situation like that and then run the bases. I saw the whole stadium going nuts, and I thought, *Now we're going to win it. There's no way we're going to lose now.*

In the 10th inning, Chipper Jones drove in the winning run with a single. I just knew we'd win that game. It's always a really good feeling to help the team win like that. Hitting that home run was really amazing, really special.

We were pretty pumped up after winning the first two games in Atlanta, and we went to Chicago and beat them pretty easily there in Game 3, 6–2, even though it was only 1–0 until we scored five in the eighth inning to sweep the series. I also threw out three of their four attempted base stealers in the series.

Then we played San Diego in the NLCS. It seemed like every other team we had faced in the playoffs—it was new and exciting for them, but it was just another year in the playoffs for us.

Everything was clicking for the Padres. They won the first three games. They had the pitching, the hitting, everything. They played well. Kevin Brown, who had been with the Marlins the year before, shut us out 3–0 in Game 2 in Atlanta. He had our number.

Ken Caminiti had a tremendous series, hitting two key home runs. Quilvio Veras was tough on us. Their catcher, Carlos Hernandez, and Steve Finley both hit over .300 and hurt us. Tony Gwynn wasn't that big of a factor, but Veras was on base a lot.

Sterling Hitchcock, a left-hander, beat Maddux 4–1 in Game 3 to give them a 3–0 lead in the series. Then we won Games 4 and 5 at San Diego to get back to Atlanta, but Hitchcock beat us again 5–0. We only got two hits, and they had 10 against Glavine and the bullpen.

We had a great year but couldn't keep it going in the playoffs. I was sick, absolutely sick. They shut down Galarraga (2-for-21), which really hurt. It's hard to win when they shut down your best hitter.

I had a home run but not much else, just singles (6-for-20, .300). Hitchcock was the MVP. He didn't have the world's greatest stuff, but we couldn't hit him. He shut us down completely. It was very frustrating. Then the Yankees swept the Padres in the World Series—and they swept us in the 1999 World Series. Damn Yankees!

We were watching the World Series at home again. I was just sick. It's not that we were missing something on the team. We didn't have a clue why this was happening, unless it was trying too much, trying too hard.

We didn't need another pitcher, another hitter, another manager, more support from the fans…none of that! We won 106 games. We had it all. Five pitchers with 16 or more wins, and we hit all those home runs too.

It was a great team, but we couldn't hit Sterling Hitchcock. We needed a break, some luck, someone to bobble a ball or something. I guess that's all we needed to win. That's how the Yankees won a lot of times.

It's sad that we didn't do better in the playoffs all those years—14 division titles and only one World Series. I should have had a lot more rings in my case instead of five (one world championship and four NL championships). At the same time, I was very fortunate to have what I had, to have been in the playoffs 11 straight years.

The 1998 season was pretty good for me (.284/34/106). Those were the numbers I knew I was capable of putting up. Those are the kind of numbers I always pictured myself having.

In 1999 I started the season in a good rhythm. I was hitting very well. I remember playing in Arizona on June 20 and feeling really good that day. I was on a hot streak, with five home runs and nine RBIs in my last six games. I'd hit in 31 of my last 39 games for a .348 average.

I'd already hit two home runs that day and then reached on a fielder's choice in the seventh inning. Darren Holmes was pitching for them. He was with us a couple of years later. I wasn't a fast runner, but I could run when I had to. He had this slow motion, and I took off on my own, and when I slid into second base, I realized the second baseman already had the ball. How did that happen? I wasn't that slow!

I got a big jump. Damian Miller, their catcher, made a perfect throw. He threw a laser to second base. I saw the second baseman with the ball, and I was trying to make a quick slide and pop up to make it look like I was safe. It makes it harder for the umpire.

But by doing that, my spikes got stuck in the dirt, and my whole body went over my knee, and I tore my ACL. I felt something pop, and I was in pain—big time.

I called for trainer Jeff Porter. I got up, but I was in pain. Bubba asked me if I was okay. I told him I felt something pop in there and it hurt like crazy. They stretched it out, and I was moving around. The pain went away. I was able to walk, but it hurt when I extended my knee completely. So, I walked without stretching it out completely.

They asked me if I could catch. It took me a while before I said I could. It was the seventh inning. I ended up finishing the game with a torn ACL. Earlier that game, Eddie Perez had played first base. They took him out of the game, and there was no other catcher. So I had to finish. I had one more at-bat and struck out. The catcher dropped the ball, but I had no intention of running. I just jogged slowly.

At one point, I knew it was really bad. Catching didn't bother me, because my leg wasn't extended. It was bent. But when someone hit a ground ball, I had to run down the line to back up first base. I did it hard at first, but I felt that pain. I started limping again because it really hurt.

It was a long day. After the game, they took X-rays and saw I had a torn ACL. They didn't know how severe it was, though, until I had surgery and they opened it up. They told me I could either have surgery right away and miss the whole season or wear a special brace and try to play through the season.

I decided to play with the brace. I spent two weeks on the disabled list and then came back July 15 and played another week and a half with the brace.

While I was playing with the brace, the doctor had to drain my knee because it was getting filled up with fluid. That had to be the most painful thing I've ever experienced. I did it three or four times. But after the first time, they numbed the area first.

The first time, Dr. Joe Chandler did it and didn't numb the area. Why he didn't numb it, I don't know. Why I agreed to it, I don't know either.

He stuck this big, thick needle in under my kneecap. Oh, my God! Every time he moved it to suck out more fluid, it was hitting all the nerves inside.

You should have seen my face. That was the most pain I've ever felt. Ask anybody how much pain I can tolerate—getting hit by a pitch, by a foul ball, by a runner…whatever. I can tolerate it. But that pain of having my knee drained, I just couldn't stand it.

The next time they told me it needed to be drained, I said, "We're not doing it until somebody numbs that up first."

When they numbed it, I felt a little pain but nothing compared to that first time. They stuck that needle in, and I was scared because of the pain I had felt the first time. But when they said it was done, I said, "What the heck was I thinking before?"

I was doing okay, but then I hit one of those swinging bunts in Philadelphia on July 24, and I ran fast. The catcher made a bad throw, and when I saw the ball go right by me, I twisted my knee when I tried to go to second.

When you have a torn ACL, everything backward and forward is okay, but once you make a pivot, you don't have any support. The two bones shift, and that's when you feel the pain. I had to pivot on that play, and we were playing on artificial turf, and I was in terrible pain. I couldn't play anymore after that and shut it down.

I had the surgery July 26, 1999, in Atlanta at Piedmont Hospital. Dr. Marvin Royster did it. When they opened it up, they saw I just had two little strings left before it would be torn completely.

I don't usually read the papers, but I did then and saw that they said a lot of catchers who have that ACL surgery come back from it. But I remember talking to Sandy Alomar back in Puerto Rico, and he said, "Don't listen to that, because I had ACL surgery and came back normal. It'll be a little uncomfortable. You'll feel a little pain, but it will go away."

That made me feel better. I was thinking about whether or not I'd have to play another position. I wish I did! But they did the surgery, and I started therapy right away. I wasn't going to let that knee affect my career. I was working my knee every single day, doing things I wasn't supposed to do, because I wanted to get better quicker.

GETTING HURT AND TAKING THE REST OF THE YEAR OFF WASN'T THE BEST THING FOR ME. The team not only won but went to the World Series, and that was very hurtful too, because I would have given anything to be playing in that World Series.

At the same time, Eddie Perez stepped in for me, and he was MVP of the NLCS! To this day, he keeps reminding everyone, "I'm Eddie Perez, 1999 NLCS MVP."

It was a tough year for me, not only because I got hurt but also because it was the year my mom passed away. It wasn't the same, playing and thinking about my mom at the same time. It was tough.

My mom was suffering from stress. My brother was on drugs. My sister was going through a divorce with Juan Gonzalez. They both were taking their issues to my parents instead of facing them themselves. They should have kept my parents away from those issues, but they involved my parents as much as they could. There were issues with me and my ex-wife too. My mom was very, very stressed, and the way she calmed down was by drinking. She used to wake up at 4:00 or 5:00 in the morning and have a beer. By 7:00 she was already feeling good. I never knew that. It was something I found out after she passed away.

She was a smoker too. She had smoked since she was 14 years old. Back then, it was no big deal. She tried to quit one time, but she never really did.

All that stress, and she had a heart issue too. She had a stroke and passed out. They did all sorts of tests on her and didn't find anything, but I guess they didn't do the crucial test to check to see if there was a blockage. They did everything else, and everything was okay.

A month or two later, she had another stroke. She called my dad and said she had that feeling again. My dad was desperate and didn't know what to do. He called the ambulance right away. They tried to revive her, but she passed away.

I was in San Diego. It was May 7. My dad didn't know how to reach me. He called Jorge Posada, the scout who had signed me. He was able to call our clubhouse and talk to one of the attendants.

It was right before the game. I was walking down to the dugout with my gear on, ready to start the game, when one of the guys yelled, "Javy! Javy! You've got a phone call from Jorge Posada in Puerto Rico. Your mom passed away."

I mean, just like that, my world was changed. I thought, *Did I hear right?* I couldn't believe what he had just told me.

I'd walked all the way down and was about to turn into the dugout. I turned around and started walking back up to the clubhouse. I realized, "This is real. There's no way I can play."

I talked with Posada on the phone, and he said, "Javy, I'm so sorry, but your mom passed away."

I was like, "No! No! No!" and started crying. I called my dad right away. He answered the phone and told me the news. I thought, *What am I going to do?* It's a long way from San Diego to Puerto Rico.

Everybody came up and told me how sorry they were. Ozzie Guillen (a Braves infielder who now manages the Marlins) was with me the whole time this was happening. I didn't play, of course.

Bill Acree, the Braves' traveling secretary, put me on a midnight flight. Paul Kinzer happened to be there in San Diego. As a friend, he decided to fly back with me. He was going to fly back the next day and was going to stay with me at the hotel that night. But once he found out what had happened, he decided to change flights and fly back with me.

My flight got into Atlanta around 6:00 in the morning, and right away, we got on a flight to Puerto Rico. I spent four or five days there, and then I flew back. My mom was only 62.

The day she died was my parents' anniversary. I remember shopping for a card because it was Mother's Day too. I bought the card in San Diego and mailed it, and it arrived the same day I got there.

My dad was the saddest person in the world. He loved my mom unconditionally. Everybody was very sad. It was the first time we had experienced someone that close to us dying.

I know that's part of life. I'm sure the one thing she'd have wanted me to do was to keep playing, to keep my career going. So I was sad, but I moved forward. She was a very sweet lady and always very supportive of me. She was very sweet and very humble, very likeable. Everyone loved her, and she got along with everyone.

She was very protective of us. She never liked to see any of us hurt. That's probably why she had a hard time with my ex-wife, Analy. My ex, my sister Elaine, and I are all around the same age, and they had this little confrontation back when we were kids in school. I don't even remember what it was about—something stupid. My mom was protecting my sister, Analy's mom was protecting her, and I was in the middle.

Analy was at our house, and my dad told Elaine to apologize. She said she was sorry for what she had done. Whether it was sincere or not, I don't know.

After that, they were on speaking terms. Unfortunately, her mom kept telling Analy that she was not liked in our family—that my parents didn't like her because of what had happened with my sister. It's hard to believe, but they took it very seriously.

My mom was protective of me in the beginning, but years later she accepted that Analy was my wife. But Analy's mom was constantly telling her things, and, of course, her mom didn't like my sister at all. My mother felt like, "If you don't like my kids, I cannot like you."

I'm pretty sure any mom would do the same thing. It's not like my mom didn't like my ex. She just didn't agree with some of the things her mother did, like the way she treated my sister and my family. It ruined our relationship, our marriage, everything.

After that, my love for Analy disappeared. We were married 11 years. She was doing whatever her mother told her to do. I would say my love for her was gone the last four or five years before we divorced.

I was with her mainly because I didn't believe in divorce. Nobody in my family had been divorced except my sister. I don't think my parents wanted to see me divorce either, but it had to be done. I'd much rather live a happy life.

It was sad for me because of my kids, but I was able to separate it from baseball. My kids were the ones suffering. My heart was broken every time I saw my kids cry as I left the house. I wished they understood why I left. It wasn't their fault. I still loved them and didn't abandon them.

In Puerto Rico, there is this television program called *La Comay*, which is a gossip show that spreads all kinds of rumors. Someone called that show and said that Javy Lopez "abandoned" his family. It was all over the news that I "abandoned" my family. I couldn't believe it.

Right away, I called Analy and said, "I don't know who said that, but I want to make it clear I didn't abandon you guys."

The divorce was finalized in 2003.

IN 2000 WE GOT KNOCKED OUT OF THE PLAYOFFS IN THE DIVISION SERIES when St. Louis swept us in three games. And 2001 wasn't much better. I got hurt on September 30 when my ankle was injured in a collision at the plate with the Mets' Robin Ventura.

I don't think he was trying to hurt me. He didn't run into me—he slid. I was positioned wrong. He slid into my left ankle, and I didn't feel much at the time. But when I started to walk back to the dugout, I felt a sharp pain. When they X-rayed it, they found a hairline fracture.

I missed the last six games of the regular season and also had to sit out the Division Series. But I came back for the NLCS.

We swept Houston in the Division Series, but then we were no match in the NLCS for Arizona's Randy Johnson and Curt Schilling, who pitched the Diamondbacks to their first World Series title.

In 2002 I had the worst year of my career (.233, 11 home runs, 52 RBIs), though I did hit my 171st career home run September 27 to pass

Braves Hall of Famer Del Crandall for the most homers by a catcher in franchise history. San Francisco sent us home in the Division Series.

My marriage was shutting down before and throughout the season. I really wasn't happy, but I was always hoping things would change for the better. That was the year the boat couldn't take any more water. I was completely unhappy. I played the season unhappy. Even though I had the two kids, I wasn't looking forward to going home. I didn't have a good season. It was like my life was falling apart.

OFF THE FIELD

MY RELATIONSHIP WITH ANALY WASN'T ALWAYS PAINFUL, OF course. We got married in 1991 when I was playing at Durham. Analy was my high school sweetheart. I met her in the ninth grade. She had transferred to my school, so she was the new girl. She was one of the prettiest girls, and everyone was talking about her.

One day at a party that a mutual friend was having, I happened to meet her. She actually came over to me and said, "Aren't you going to say hi?" I couldn't believe she did that, so I said, "Hi!" and introduced myself. We wound up talking the whole night.

I was shy, but once she started the conversation, I was fine. I never would have approached her. She was very attractive, and I was intimidated. But since she came up to me, we talked and danced all night.

The day after the party she came up to me and started talking, and she made me feel more comfortable. We started getting closer to each other and eventually became boyfriend and girlfriend. I wouldn't say I went out on a true "date" with her, because 99 percent of the time, her mom was with us.

Back in high school, there were school parties at different places around the city. We would all be aware of when and where the next party would be. In school, she said, "Are you going to go to that party?"

This was before we were boyfriend and girlfriend. I told her I'd like to go, and she said, "We'd like to give you a ride."

I said, "Sure," and her mom picked me up at home and we went to the party. The relationship started getting deeper, and we started dating. The dating was pretty much the same as before—we'd go to these parties.

We were still kissing on the cheek at this point. Then one day, she pulled her head out of the car, and I was going to kiss her on the cheek. But she turned around, and I accidentally kissed her on the mouth. Her mother was there, and I was very embarrassed. Actually, her mother seemed like she'd been looking forward to that. But I wasn't, because I was shy!

Our relationship was pretty much like that for the next six years. I mean, for six years, her mother was with us all the time. For some families in Puerto Rico, that was normal, but for the majority of families, it was not like that.

Usually, at a certain age, the mother gives the girl some freedom, but her mother wouldn't let go. She was very, very protective. At the age of 18 or 19, we were going out alone more often. But the first four years of our relationship, she was with us all the time.

She finally let go once Analy started college. But even though we went out alone, she always needed to be back by midnight. The relationship continued. I signed with the Braves when I was 17, and Analy and I had been dating for three years. It was hard for me and for her to be apart for seven months.

I told her when I was 18 or 19 that I wanted her to come and visit me while I was playing in the United States. But, of course, her mother would never, ever let her travel to the States to visit me. Obviously she feared the worst. She was afraid Analy would get pregnant.

Every teammate's girlfriend came to visit him. I thought it was pretty cool. I thought it was a way to prolong the relationship. At the same time, it was also a way for the couples to determine if they were right for each other.

Eventually I felt like I had no other choice…the only way Analy could come to the States was if we got married. Talk about pressure! But since she was the only girlfriend I'd had since I was 14 years old, I didn't know any different.

We decided to get married during the 1991 season. She was 19, and I was 20. She had to finish college in May. I flew from Durham to Puerto Rico after a game to get married. There were 100 to 150 people at the wedding. We got married at the same church where I went to school and met her: Colegio Mercedario San Judas Tadeo. Two or three days later, I flew back and met the team in Lynchburg. That's pretty much where we spent our honeymoon—Lynchburg, Virginia.

A lot of things changed after we got married. At the beginning, it was the best thing ever. Then, year after year, it got tougher. The biggest difference came when my first son, Javy, was born in 1995. Analy became more strict and wanted more attention for our son, and I could understand that. It was the best feeling in the world when Javy was born—the birth of my first child.

We were enjoying having the baby, but as he got older, things started to change. The relationship wasn't the same. Kelvin, our second son, was born in 1999. I noticed the love had gone out of our marriage. I was living a life with her where there wasn't any love. We didn't tell each other "I love you" anymore.

We'd still hold hands and things like that, but the love wasn't there. I was enjoying being by myself more than being around her. Because of the lack of love in the relationship, I wasn't interested in doing things around the house. Normally, I like to keep things organized. But after a while I didn't care how we lived.

Thinking back, I feel so bad that I never helped her do dishes, clean the house, and do things around the house. If I'd have been in love, I would have helped her do everything, but the relationship was falling apart. I thought I was going to live like that for the rest of my life.

I'm not the kind of guy who likes confrontation. I always try to avoid it. Unfortunately, I kept my mouth shut for a couple of years. I knew I was doing the wrong thing, because I could see myself becoming a worse and worse husband. I felt bad, but at the same time, I didn't have any motivation to be any better.

It just got worse, and then one day in 2002, after I had my worst season, I was super miserable. I had two beautiful boys, a beautiful home, and a nice car, but everywhere I looked, everything was making me unhappy. I felt like I needed to do something, but I still was avoiding confrontation. I was completely miserable. I didn't say much to Analy.

Whenever she'd ask, "What's wrong with you?" I'd say, "Nothing."

Finally, I told her, "I want to be honest with you. I am completely unhappy."

She said, "Why?"

I didn't want to give her a reason. I just told her I was unhappy and didn't know why. That was 2002. She was trying to make it better, but nothing helped. We even went on a vacation, which was something we had never done.

She booked a trip to Atlantis in the Bahamas. It was fun, because we were out of the ordinary routine and I saw my kids enjoying themselves. Prior to that, we didn't go anywhere. In the off-season, we'd just go to Puerto Rico, because we began living full-time in Atlanta in 2000 when Javy started school.

Right after that trip to the Bahamas, we went to Aspen, Colorado. Again, it made me feel a little better, but it was just temporary relief. We had some fun on our trips. We did something we hadn't done before. The kids had a blast, and it was fun to see that. But when we came back, everything was still the same. I returned to reality. That's when I said, "That's it."

When Analy came to spring training in 2003, I felt bad, because she came with the kids, and her sister was with her. Thank God her sister came, because she was able to talk to her most of the time, as I didn't have much to say. She felt that. The day she had to leave, I took them to the airport. I kissed the kids, and I was going to kiss her, but before I did, she said, "Don't even bother. Don't worry about it."

I said, "Okay."

Her sister, who lives in Miami, had already left. Analy said she knew that week was bad, that I didn't make it a good week. Anyway, she went back home with the kids. We talked a few times. I told her I was unhappy, and she said not to bother coming home after spring training.

When spring training was over, I went back to Atlanta and went straight to the apartment I had in Buckhead. I got a phone message the next day from her lawyer that said she had filed for divorce.

Even though I talked with Analy a few times about trying to make things work, I knew I'd crossed the point of no return. It didn't matter what she said or did. My mind was already set. I wish I had told her, "Don't even bother." Giving her any false hope just made things more painful for her.

She told me to call her one night to talk while the kids were sleeping. I told her I felt like we got married too early. We didn't have much of a relationship before we got married. I felt like I had missed out on a lot by being married at the age of 20.

I didn't want to see a counselor, because I already knew what I wanted. But I said I'd do it, and we went to see one. That made it worse, because I didn't even give the counselor a chance to work with me. I just said my mind was made up.

So the counselor told Analy how I felt, and she said, "Okay" and left. I hated to see the suffering, but at the same time, I said, "This is what it is. This is what divorce is about. We both suffer, but in the end, we'll be happier."

We're both Catholic. I felt bad because of that, but everything has changed since then. You live and learn. The way I see religion now is totally different. It's like politics. So many religions. So many beliefs. Where is the truth? I believe what I want to believe. No more believing what other people want me to believe.

I went back to Atlanta to start the season. Analy's attorney sent me the divorce papers, and we started the divorce settlement, which continued throughout the whole year.

She did everything she could to work it out, but in the end, she said, "Have a nice life."

I said, "Sorry, but thank you." And then I left.

I hoped we'd still be friends, because we had two kids together and we had been married for 11 years. And before that, we had dated for six years. I never disrespected her. I don't think I ever even swore at her. My parents taught me good manners. I always respect people. I was just honest with her and told her how I felt.

Unfortunately, ever since that day, she hasn't wanted to have anything to do with me. She has gotten past it to some extent, but she still doesn't want to be friends.

I REMARRIED A YEAR AND A HALF LATER. I didn't expect to marry again, at least not that soon. But what I was looking for came quickly.

I met Gina through a mutual friend in San Francisco at the end of 2002. She was working for a computer software company. The Braves were out there playing against the Giants.

Her friend was friends with Orlando Cepeda Jr., the son of the great Hall of Fame player. He invited me to this restaurant called MoMo's, which is right across the street from the stadium in San Francisco. Orlando introduced me to several of his friends, including Gina. When I saw Gina, I thought, *Wow!* But we all just talked in a group, and only later did I have a conversation with just her.

I was still married to Analy, though our relationship was basically over. I was miserable, but when I met Gina, she was so sweet and kind. I gave her my email address because she was going to send me some jokes that she had gotten from friends. So she sent me things during that winter. I was already in Puerto Rico, and I was having the toughest time. My marriage was getting worse and worse and worse.

I started telling Gina more about my relationship. We were just friends. She had no interest in being with me because she knew I was married. We liked each other, but we were just friends. She was willing to listen and to try to help me. She said the most important thing in life is to be happy. She was like my psychologist. When I was down and struggling, I told her what was happening.

We talked on the phone too, and I started having feelings for her. I thought, *Where were you all these years?* She got me. She's just a cool person. I could see myself ending up with her for many, many reasons.

In August 2003 the Braves were playing in San Francisco, and I was really looking forward to seeing Gina again. It was just a three-game series, but we saw each other and talked and hung out. After that, it started to become more of a relationship, and we were seeing each other more and more.

I was legally separated and going through my divorce. I didn't know if or how seeing Gina would affect the settlement, so we were just friends until December, when the divorce was final. Then I pretty much made it official that she was my girlfriend, and she moved to Atlanta to be with me. I told her we couldn't continue being so far apart and asked her to pack up and live with me.

It was a big, big decision for her. She has a degree in English Literature from Cal State–San Bernardino, had a good job with an e-commerce company, and was making decent money. She had worked hard all her life to get where she was. But looking at the big picture, she could see we couldn't keep living so far apart or else we'd wind up being just friends again.

Her family was in Ontario, California, and she was in San Francisco, so she already was several hours away from them. Her dad was pretty concerned about her moving to Atlanta to live with a ballplayer, and I didn't blame him.

It took her a while to make her decision, but she finally gave up her job and her apartment and moved to Atlanta. I really admire her for what she did. It was a big step. California to Georgia—she wasn't happy about the difference in weather. She had to deal with my ex and with my kids, who at that point hadn't learned their manners the way they should have. I blame myself for that because I hadn't been with them much in the previous couple of years.

When Gina finally moved in with me, I learned that Analy had told the kids all kinds of stuff about me. She told Kelvin something that made him say he didn't want to be with me as long as Gina was in the house. At three years old, I'm sure he didn't come up with that on his own. He didn't even know Gina. He said, "Is Gina there? I don't want to go!"

One day we all sat down and talked—me, Gina, and the two boys. We told them how things were going to be from then on: "This is the way it is. Gina's not going anywhere."

But Analy kept telling them, "You don't have to stay there, because they're not married. You don't have to be with your dad. You come back home every day."

So whenever I had the kids, I had to take them back the same day. The following day, I had to pick them up and then take them back at the end of that day. Three, four days in a row. It was a pain. I was in Buckhead, and she was out in the suburbs. It was 35 minutes one way, every day, just because Gina was staying with me.

Analy got away with that, but do you think she was thinking about the kids? Do you think the kids were happy to take that ride back and forth every day? I don't think so, but Analy was happy about it because it was hard on me.

For some reason I was having a great season despite everything that was going on off the field. If I had a bad game, I felt like I had an excuse. I was going through a divorce. I guess that's what I had in my mind. If I was 0-for-4, I had an excuse. But at the same time, that motivated me, and I happened to have the best season of my career.

Because it was hard for Gina to be in Atlanta, I bought a house in La Jolla in 2004 because her dream was to live in Southern California. I was making good money, and I wanted to please her. Then I was going back and forth every time I could to see the kids.

We planned to get married in February 2005. In 2004 we pretty much had everything set—the hotel, the dress. But in May Gina got pregnant. We talked about it, and she didn't want to get married when she was visibly pregnant. So we moved up the wedding.

We went from planning a big wedding to having a quick wedding with just her and me and her mom and dad during the season in Baltimore. We got married on June 23, 2004, at a nondenominational church in downtown Baltimore. It went pretty smoothly. It was funny. We didn't have anything planned or reserved, so we were taking pictures in the terrace patio of this residence hotel where we were staying. Everything was cool, and slowly we started moving into the hotel.

At one point, we had cameras everywhere inside the hotel, and the hotel manager came over and asked, "What's going on around here? In order to take pictures in the hotel, you need to pay." We didn't know that. It was pretty embarrassing, but at the same time, we took all the pictures before they said anything. They turned out pretty good!

A week or two before the wedding, Gina had a miscarriage. We'd already cancelled everything we had set up for 2005, so when she had the miscarriage, we asked ourselves, "Do we have to cancel everything again?" We decided to go ahead and get married.

It was devastating for Gina when she had the miscarriage. I didn't realize all she had to go through. She actually started the miscarriage as I was leaving for the ballpark to take the bus to catch a flight to Chicago. I didn't know what was happening to her. We went to the hospital that morning, and then I left and took off for the road trip. I didn't know whether to stay or go. I didn't know what to tell the team, because she was my girlfriend, not my wife. I didn't know if they would care about me not going to Chicago with the team.

She was by herself at the hospital, getting all sorts of things done to her. She was by herself crying, and I left for Chicago. I tried to talk to her on the phone, but she didn't want to talk to me. She was mad that I had left her there by herself. I felt bad about it. I should have stayed there with her and said the heck with the game. But I just didn't know what to do at the time.

But we got married, and I was able to tell Javy and Kelvin, "Listen, now you can stay with me!"

After that, Gina had doubts about whether or not she wanted to have kids. Even before the miscarriage, she didn't think she wanted to have a baby. But she changed her mind and was very happy about getting pregnant, and I was too.

After the miscarriage, we decided just to enjoy life and not try to have kids. I already had two. The first four years we were married, we just did things together, traveled, and enjoyed life.

I actually became a dad, a totally different dad, to Javy and Kelvin. Gina has been the best stepmom anyone could have. It's hard for her because she's not their mother, but she respects them to the max, and the kids see that. They love Gina.

In our fifth year of marriage, we started to think about having kids again. But she couldn't get pregnant. We tried all the usual methods to get pregnant, but nothing worked for almost two years. I felt bad. I already had two boys, but we wanted to have our own kids too, and it just wasn't working.

There was a point when she gave up. But her mother or someone talked her out of it, and then she decided to try in-vitro fertilization. We tried the first round and said, "If we don't get pregnant here, we're never going to get pregnant."

But the first time we tried—negative. We couldn't believe it. We were starting to think about possibly adopting a baby.

We talked to a lot of people after that, and so many of them said it wasn't until after their second or third or fifth round that they got pregnant. Not many get pregnant the first time.

So Gina gave herself another chance, and the second time she got pregnant with Brody. It was life-changing. We cannot go anywhere now!

Regardless of where we go, there's always a lot of packing for the baby and upsetting his routine—eat, play, sleep. When I went to spring training as an instructor with the Braves in 2011, I thought Gina was going with me. But at the last minute, she decided not to go because of Brody.

At spring training, I was off every day at noon. I wasn't planning to play golf every day, but I had to do something, so I took my clubs and played every day. Maybe Gina and Brody can make it next time!

TEAMMATES

THE FIRST TIME I MET BOBBY COX WAS IN PUERTO RICO WHEN HE came to see me play. I just met him briefly. He was the general manager back then. It was 1987, and I had signed with the Braves.

Then in 1990, when I was at Class A in Burlington, Iowa, he became the Braves manager in the middle of the season. Back then, I just knew he was doing a good job. I didn't know he'd been a manager before that (1978–81 in Atlanta and 1982–85 in Toronto).

I don't remember much about 1990 except the Braves were in last place, and one night the lights went out for a couple of hours at Atlanta-Fulton County Stadium. It was just a terrible season. We didn't have the best season at Burlington either, though we had a pretty good record and still finished third.

In 1991 it was fun watching the Braves as the whole Tomahawk Era started. It was interesting to see Bobby managing the team. Coming into spring training in 1992, I saw Bobby as a totally different person from the man I had known before as general manager. I wasn't on the big-league roster in 1991, but in 1992 I came up to the majors and I saw Bobby again for the third or fourth time since I signed.

Since day one, I saw Bobby as a guy who knew how to get players' respect. After I left the Braves in 2003, I saw how other managers worked with players, and I started to compare them to Bobby. There was no comparison.

Bobby wasn't too personal with the players, but the few things he said to us might be what we'd hear from our dads. He showed nothing but concern for us. That's how I compared Bobby to other managers.

I didn't realize how good Bobby was until I left the Braves. The reason he was so good is that he knew how to handle the players. He always showed that. If he had to be thrown out of games 158 times to protect players, he'd do it. Not many managers do that for the players.

The guy had his routine. He always got to the ballpark early for all those years. As far as I know, he never changed his routine. If things worked for him, he would never change anything.

Was he superstitious? I don't know. Maybe that's why he always wore spikes. Those aren't the most comfortable shoes for someone to walk around in. He always said he was more comfortable in spikes. I don't know how that could be, but it was part of his tradition. He kept it all the way until the end. He wanted to feel like a player, and he did it.

He was always focused on baseball—breakfast, lunch, and dinner was baseball! Everybody loved him. I don't think he ever had to pay for a meal. He probably did, but he didn't have to! He got everything for free because he was so famous. Everybody knew him, and everybody loved him.

For those who played a lot of years for Bobby, he represented the father in the family. If he had something to tell the players, he'd always delegate it to the coaches to do—Pat Corrales or Ned Yost. The good thing about Pat and Ned is they knew how to approach the players in a way that wasn't offensive or disrespectful.

It was easy to gain Bobby's confidence. He was not the kind of person who would talk to you about how he felt. But if something bothered him, he let Corrales know, and Corrales knew how to approach a player without making him feel bad.

That was something I always admired about Pat. He never hurt your feelings. He always came to me in a way where I knew they wanted me to succeed and they wanted to help me. Not in a way like, "You better do this or your ass is out of there." It was, "Javy, we need you. You're really important to this team."

The way Bobby would stand in the dugout and cheer for the players showed us that he cared about the game and that he wasn't just there to collect paychecks. We knew his heart and soul were in the game and that he was in our corner. He was there because he loved the game. It was his job, and he worked hard and showed people how hard he was working. He wanted to show he couldn't be replaced, and he wasn't replaced until he decided to retire.

I'd tell Bobby, "That pitch was a strike. The umpire is terrible," and he'd pretty much attack the umpire right away. Umpires wound up getting mad at me for telling Bobby. They knew Bobby had a bad temper, and they would all tell me, "Don't tell Bobby!"

I don't know if he really had a bad temper, but baseball was that important to him. Of course, he was friends with all the umpires after the game. Before and after the game, they would speak, but during the game, he was all over them.

That was just part of the job for Bobby. Being around Bobby, I heard him argue with the umpire right next to me, and I learned every cuss word there is—and then some! I heard it all from him arguing with umpires.

A lot of times, though, Bobby got thrown out without saying anything bad or offensive to the umpire. That always made me mad. Then after getting thrown out, he would decide to get his money's worth and get thrown out the right way. That's when he'd use all the cuss words.

A lot of times he got thrown out unnecessarily. I guess the fans expected it, so the umpires did it out of routine. I've seen a lot of other managers say a lot worse things to the umpire than Bobby and not get thrown out. It always amazed me.

I never got thrown out of a game. I got a warning twice. Once I struck out—called—and threw the helmet as hard as I could on the ground. Bobby came out right away and said, "Stop. Don't do that." He backed me up and talked to the umpire right away.

The other time I got called out on strikes on a fastball in. I was so mad that I drew a line where the ball went in front of the umpire. Bobby came out and said, "Don't ever do that!" But I was pissed. He called me out on a fastball that was way inside, and I showed the umpire exactly where the ball went. I didn't get thrown out, but I pissed off the umpire, and he didn't give us good calls the rest of the night.

I never saw Bobby break down after a tough loss, but he always got really, really mad. When we lost because a player didn't hustle, he never said anything to the player. The player would feel like crap, would know it was his fault, and Bobby didn't say anything to him. I respect Bobby for that. He just went to his office, closed the door, and all you heard was him throwing things and swearing!

It would always be the following day that he would call someone into his office. He'd wait until he cooled down. Then he'd have a coach go get whoever it was he wanted to talk to. Ned Yost came up to me a few times, and Pat Corrales too. A lot of times it would be to ask questions like, "On the home run last night, did the pitcher shake you off the slider? Did you call that pitch?" Bobby wanted to know whose fault it was—the pitcher's or mine. I'd say, "I called that pitch, but it wasn't where I wanted it" or, "I wanted to call a different pitch, but he shook me off."

He hated it when a rookie pitcher shook me off and then gave up a home run. The team philosophy was getting people out outside. When we gave up a home run on a fastball inside, Bobby and pitching coach Leo Mazzone were pissed. Nobody wanted to see Leo pissed off either. He was just as frightening as Bobby.

Bobby used Pat and Ned throughout my career to deliver messages to players. When Bobby couldn't take any more was when somebody didn't hustle.

I remember one time that I didn't run on a pop fly. I was frustrated. When I got back to the dugout, all I heard was, "You've got to fucking hustle! Shit! Fuck!"

But I didn't hear him very well, and I looked at him and said, "What?" because I didn't know what he had said. He didn't repeat it. He just kept looking at me as mad as he could be and saying, "Fuck! Fuck!" Then someone—I think it might have been Rafael Belliard—pushed me down and said, "Just sit down, Javy! You didn't hustle."

I said, "That's true. I deserve it."

That probably was the only time he got mad at me. If he got mad at me other times, I never saw it, which is good.

Leo was a lot like Bobby. He also had his philosophy and his routine. He became famous with that pitching rotation. Who wouldn't? But he had a good philosophy, and he knew how to teach pitchers. He had a lot of knowledge about pitching. He knew what he was doing. He knew what every pitcher was doing wrong. If a pitcher wasn't honest with him, he could tell. He'd get more frustrated and disappointed, because he always wanted the pitchers to be honest. If a guy was hurt or just didn't have his good stuff, Leo wanted to know. The more information you could give him, the better he would coach you.

He'd get just as pissed as Bobby in the dugout. Bobby would be swearing at the umpire, and Leo would be just as mad. Bobby would say something, and then Leo would say something. Bobby would protect all his players and pitchers. Leo would protect his pitchers just as much. He got thrown out a few times because he defended his pitchers to the limit. He cared about them and made sure they did their work.

We had some fun with him and the way he "rocked" on the bench. We called him "the Penguin." I remember some players counted how many times he'd rock during the game. It was thousands of times!

But I respected him a lot. He is a man of strong character, and that's what made him a very good pitching coach.

Leo wasn't happy when he went to Baltimore. He couldn't wait to leave the Orioles. The organization was such a mess. Going from Atlanta to that, it was miserable. Leo left the Braves after 2005 for a three-year deal in Baltimore. That didn't go well, and the Orioles fired him after two years, with one more year left on his contract.

Now he's working for a radio station in Atlanta, and he's doing awesome. I'm happy for him.

THE FIRST MEMORY I HAVE OF ANDRES GALARRAGA comes from when I was a rookie in spring training at West Palm Beach. The Expos trained there too, along with the Braves.

Melvin Nieves had the guts to go into the Expos' big-league clubhouse looking for a batting glove, and I was stupid enough to follow him. All these players were getting dressed, changing for the game. Melvin talked to Junior Noboa, who said he didn't have any but to "ask Galarraga. He's a nice guy."

We go up to him, and I didn't even know how to pronounce his name.

"Hey, Galarraga, I'm Javy Lopez," I said. I was so embarrassed. "You don't happen to have a pair of batting gloves, do you?"

"Yeah, yeah. Take those," he said, handing me a pair of used batting gloves.

When we left, I said, "Melvin, don't you ever, ever, ever do that to me again."

So I got a pair of batting gloves from Big Cat. I told him the story when he came to the Braves. It was funny, because Galarraga's batting glove was really big on me. His hand had stretched it way out.

When I see Galarraga now, I still remind him, but he doesn't remember. He's had so many people ask him for batting gloves!

I really started watching Galarraga and following his stats after that. He did well with the Expos and then went to the Cardinals. I thought the year with St. Louis in 1992 might be the last one of his career, because he only hit .243. But then he signed with Colorado in 1993. When the season started, the Rockies were the talk of baseball—how unbelievable their hitting was. Galarraga won the batting title by hitting .370!

He had five great years there and then came to the Braves in 1998. It was all because he changed his stance and started hitting wide open. He said Don Baylor changed his stance. Baylor was a great hitting coach for some guys but not for me. He was the Braves' hitting coach in 1999. He probably didn't know how to teach me, or he couldn't figure out what my problem was. He was a great guy, and I really enjoyed being around him. I liked him a lot.

The best hitting coach I ever had—and he didn't last long with the Braves for some reason—was Merv Rettenmund. He was a hardworking guy and lived in the batting cages with the guys.

If you asked, "Where's Merv?" the answer was always, "He's in the batting cage." He was there waiting for someone to work with. He didn't go to players—the players knew he was there if they needed help. He'd talk to you first and then start working with you. That way he knew what was wrong, what was bothering you. I loved the guy. He was a great coach. T.P.—Terry Pendleton—came a few years later.

We were all happy when we heard Galarraga was going to be with the Braves in 1998. We thought he'd replace Fred McGriff, who had gone to Tampa Bay. He was the most down-to-earth guy you could ever meet.

He was like me in that he had a hard time saying no to people. He'd rather concentrate on baseball, but he didn't like to disappoint people. Everybody loved him. Not only was he very likeable in the clubhouse, but he could still rake too! His home runs were fun to watch, because they were bombs. He was so big and strong that when he hit the ball, the ball screamed.

We played a full season with him, and the same thing happened—we didn't make it to the World Series. After it was over, I told him how much I enjoyed having him on the team and was looking forward to having him there again the next season.

Then right before spring training started, the Braves announced that he had non-Hodgkin's lymphoma. We had been all pumped up about having him on the team again. When we heard this news, we didn't know how serious it was. I thought maybe it was something where he could get a few treatments and then come back. Unfortunately, he missed the whole season.

I remember some of the players wanted everyone to shave their heads in honor of Galarraga. Eddie Perez started it, I think. I told Eddie, "I love

you so much and Galarraga so much, but I'm not going to shave my head!"
A lot of players said the same thing. "We love the guy, but we're not going
to shave our heads!"

We all prayed for him, and we all called him a lot. He probably got
an individual call from everyone on the team, which is something that's
unheard of—every single person. Sometimes there would be five, six,
seven players standing there waiting for their turn to talk to him and tell
him how much we were thinking of him and praying for him and his
family. He was very grateful to have good teammates like that.

It was a big hole in our clubhouse when he couldn't be with us that
year. Ryan Klesko played first base, and we made miracles happen again—
losing a player like that and still finishing first. I was gone half the season
too, with a torn ACL. Gerald Williams played left field for Klesko, and he
did a really good job.

When we played a spring-training game in Jupiter in March 1999, we
all decided to visit Galarraga at his house in West Palm Beach. It was a
big surprise, because he didn't know we were coming. Bobby Cox and the
whole team were there. I know it meant a lot to him. He was very happy to
see us. His wife was crying.

Every time we played the Marlins down there, I always rented an
exotic car, a convertible or something. I remember I arranged for a Jaguar
once. When we got to Miami, though, I went to get the Jaguar, and they
said, "We don't have the Jaguar ready because the last guy hasn't returned
it yet."

This was a very exotic car rental place, right across the street from the
hotel where we were staying. The guy said, "You know what? Because the
car is not here yet, you can use this one." It was a blue Lamborghini!

I said, "You've got to be kidding me, right?"

We had an off day, so I took the car and went to the hotel to call Eddie
Perez. I said, "Come down here and let's go visit Galarraga."

When he came down and saw the Lamborghini, he said, "No way!"

I said, "Let's rock 'n' roll!"

It was wild, and it was fun being in that car, but it was an hour and 10
minutes with that loud engine right in back of my head.

We spent the whole day with Galarraga in his house, just hanging
out with him by the pool. Eddie really liked Big Cat and became very
good friends with him. We had a great time that day. He had so much

memorabilia, so many trophies and plaques from all over the world at his home. He accomplished a lot of things and had a great career.

When the season was over, Galarraga invited Analy and me to Venezuela for his daughter's 15th birthday—her Quinceanera. He put on a big party in Caracas. Ozzie Guillen was there. Eddie was there.

Big Cat came back in 2000 at age 39 and had another great year—a .302 average, 28 homers, and 100 RBIs. Everywhere we went, he got a big standing ovation for battling cancer and coming back. He was tipping his cap everywhere we went. In his third at-bat on Opening Day at Turner Field, he hit a home run and won the game for us. He hit six home runs in the first two weeks and was leading the league in home runs in May and made the All-Star team.

That was the last year of his contract. During the winter, I called Eddie to see what was going on and if Galarraga would be back. Then I heard on the news that the Braves had offered Galarraga a contract and he had rejected it.

I said, "No! Come on, Galarraga."

Then I found out that the Braves had offered him a low salary for one year. Yes, he missed a whole year because of cancer, but is that all he deserved after the monster year he had put up in 1998 and what he had done when he came back in 2000? It was an insult, and that's why he rejected it.

Texas then gave him $6 million. They traded him to San Francisco in the middle of the season. He hit .256 for the year with 17 home runs and 69 RBIs at age 40. You just don't make a lowball offer to a player like Galarraga after the season he had in 2000 for the Braves.

Obviously, age didn't help his contract situation, but after what he did at age 39, come on. The guy still had it, and I'm sure he would have hit even better if he'd stayed in Atlanta, because he felt comfortable there. He felt at home. All of a sudden, he had to go to the American League, and then he got traded too. It's not the same when you're going from one place to another. You want to be settled to feel comfortable.

Whatever the Braves' offer was, he said in the media he felt insulted.

I HEARD CHIPPER JONES' NAME A LOT WHEN I WAS PLAYING IN THE MINOR LEAGUES. I was always curious to see what kind of player he was. I'd try to sneak a look at him in spring training in West Palm Beach whenever I could. I looked at his swing, and everything was uppercut, uppercut. I was surprised. I wasn't that impressed with his batting practice. I said, "Wait a second. This is the first-round pick?"

But, of course, that was just one batting practice. The same year he signed, I was playing in Burlington. All the talk was about Chipper and how good he was doing in the minors. His first full year was 1991, and he had a big year at Macon. He was raking.

The following year, I saw the real Chipper taking batting practice. And playing with him in spring training, I could see he had all the tools.

I really found out how good of a player he was in 1992 when he got called up to Greenville, where I was playing. He was unbelievable. He hit .346 that second half at Greenville. Then the following year, we both played at Richmond, and he was doing the exact same thing.

Then his first year in the big leagues, we were playing the Yankees in spring training at Ft. Lauderdale. He was running to first base and pulled up because he hurt his knee. That was a real bummer, because he missed all of 1994 with a torn ACL.

He came back in 1995, and he was ready to go. I never pictured him being a power hitter, but every year he came to spring training stronger and stronger. I said, "How big is he going to get?" because when I first saw him, he was a skinny kid. "He's going to wind up hitting a lot of home runs one of these days," I said.

He could have hit a lot more homers if he had wanted, but he had always wanted to balance his power hitting with his average. When I got hurt in 1999, he and I each had around 11 or 12 home runs. Since we didn't have Galarraga, I was trying to be competitive with him, and that's the year he hit 45 home runs and won the National League MVP.

Chipper was a very interesting guy. You never knew what kind of mood he was going to bring to the clubhouse on any given day. There were days when he wouldn't even say hi to anyone…and then there were days he was kissing the batboys! You never knew what to expect, but he was always focused on baseball. He'd always try to find a way to get better, always looking for anything he was doing wrong as a player.

And he had the best instructor anyone could ask for when he got into a slump: his dad. All he did was make a phone call to his dad, and the next day, his dad was there. Whatever he said to him worked because Chipper wound up raking!

Everybody was always happy to see Chipper's dad, because we knew that meant Chipper would start hitting again. He'd start killing the ball every time his dad showed up.

There was a time when I said to him, "Why do you even let your dad go home? Keep him here with you!"

And Chipper just laughed. He had so much fame so young that it probably got into his head. He was a guy who needed to find his peace sometime, because the media and everyone else were always on top of him. He was such a valuable player.

The reporters looked at him as one of the leaders. Everywhere he went, someone wanted a piece of him. He even had a radio show where, every day, Braves broadcaster Joe Simpson was talking to him—"Chipper Diary" or something like that. I told him one day, "I don't know how you do it."

Sometimes I just had to hide from the media because I wanted peace. I wanted to concentrate on the game and stay focused. But before every game, Simpson would take Chipper aside and start talking. He did it and didn't complain.

Expectations have been high on Chipper his whole life, so it probably was very stressful to try to meet those expectations. We always got along. We weren't the best of friends. We didn't hang out together. Chipper was a very independent guy and was very selective about who he hung out with. I totally respected him for that. I always respected him as a teammate. We talked a lot, and we always got along.

WHEN I CAME UP TO THE BIG LEAGUES, Ryan Klesko is the guy I hung out with most of the time. We lived together with the same friend—Paul Kinzer. I think there was a time when Klesko was a little jealous that I was friends with his friend and he had to share everything with me.

But Klesko respected me—or tried to! We always got along. We ate together. We hung out together. We came up together at Richmond, so we've known each other for a long time. I got to know his dad, his mother, and his sister. They are a very sweet family. He was the only "beanhead."

I hunted with him one time, which is the worst thing I've ever done. It was my first time hunting. Klesko was just getting introduced to it too. Kinzer met the Tim Graham family in Dublin, Georgia, and they owned a construction company. They were very wealthy and owned something like 7,000 acres around Dublin.

Kinzer called me one day and told me about this family and their property and that they had invited us to hunt. I guess Klesko had already been there once before, and they invited me this time. We hunted for deer and wild hog—whichever came first!

First of all, they hunt at night. I think it was illegal, but since they owned the land, we didn't have to worry about it. We were in a Jeep with an upper stand or rack. Since it was my first time hunting, I had the honor of being the first shooter.

Kinzer was to my left, and Klesko was to my right. The two guys who owned the land were driving and checking with the spotlight.

We finally saw a wild boar. I was aiming at it in the bushes...but it kept moving. I knew what it was, and I didn't want to miss. The spotlight was right there. All I saw was a small portion of the hide, but I didn't know what part of the body it was. I wanted to be sure I hit it in the right area.

I was waiting and waiting, and Paul said, "What are you doing? Shoot it. It's right there!"

I said, "I know. I'm just waiting to get a better shot at it." Then as soon as I got the shot I wanted, *BOOM!* Klesko shot before me! Right in my ear. I was deaf for a week. And he missed! It was a disaster! He missed. I didn't have my first shot. The pig ran away! I had to wait for another chance.

So we looked for another pig or deer. We found more pigs, and this time they were running. I shot, and as soon as I did, again, *BOOM!* in my ear.

"Dude!" I yelled.

First of all, he was too close to me. What was he doing so close to me? He was a beanhead—a knucklehead!

This time I shot the pig in the butt. But, of course, Klesko said it was his shot. We started arguing. "I got it first!" Eventually I got credit for it. Even Paul was telling everyone I shot my first pig in the ass.

Everything you kill is cleaned and put in the freezer, and they give away all the meat for free to the people in the town because they know hunting is a hobby. They put it on a hook, cleaned it up, and everything went into the freezer. Nothing was wasted.

Another time we went dove hunting. I was on one side of the field, and Klesko was on the other. The rule is that when someone screams, "Low bird," nobody shoots. But, of course, for Klesko, "Low bird" means "Shoot!"

We were right across the field from each other. I screamed "Low bird," and he shot! All the BBs from his shotgun came right at Paul and me. I got hit by his buckshot, and it hurt! Those things sting—big time—even though we weren't that close.

But you just have to laugh at him. He thought he was the best hunter ever!

His family had been hunting for 30 or 40 years. In their house, they had a big collection of guns. Well, Klesko bought 20, 30 guns, one after another. But rather than have them in a rack, they were all thrown in the basement at Kinzer's house! He was sloppy…Klesko being Klesko. That was him.

I hunted for a couple of years with them. The last time I hunted, I killed a big pig. Then I saw about seven little piggies crying because I had just killed their mom. I didn't see them before I shot. The little ones were in the bushes. I dropped it right there, and when I was walking closer, we saw all the little ones.

My heart just dropped. I felt so bad. I said I didn't need that anymore and decided not to go back.

Klesko wasn't there that day, but you know who was? Emmanuel Lewis—the actor who starred on the TV show *Webster*. I almost got shot, because he was in a stand waiting for something to move. I was walking and trying to be sure he saw my orange vest. When I got close to him, he said, "I almost shot you! I saw something moving and then I saw your legs." I said, "Thank you for not shooting!" That was an even better reason not to hunt anymore.

Klesko was a very impressive player. I wasn't impressed the first time I saw Chipper take bating practice, but it was totally the opposite with Klesko. When I saw him hitting, he put on a show. Out of the first 15 pitches, he probably hit 12 out of the park. Bombs! His swing was hard every time.

I said, "This guy is a beast!" He was already big and strong. Very, very impressive. Not only did he hit for power, but he could hit for average.

It was interesting watching him play first base in 1999 when Galarraga was sick. That wasn't his position. He did the best he could. For his size, he ran very well. He was fast and knew how to steal bases (23 in both 2000 and 2001). He was a good base runner.

In the outfield he was good, but his arm wasn't that great, maybe because he hurt it as a pitcher before he was drafted. I think the American

League would have been a perfect fit for him as a DH, but I don't know if he'd have liked being a DH. He probably wouldn't have enjoyed all the sitting and waiting for the next at-bat.

I saw him at Tom Glavine's induction into the Braves Hall of Fame in 2010. He hasn't changed. He finally got married. He's got a new baby.

It's funny because when I left the Braves Hall of Fame ceremony, I looked in my rearview mirror, and there was a police car with the lights flashing and the siren on. I looked closer—and it was Klesko driving the police car, siren going! Unbelievable!

KLESKO AND I WENT TO CURACAO IN THE WINTER OF 1994 to do some clinics. Among all the kids, Andruw Jones was there. He'd already signed with the Braves. We were eating at an Applebee's, and he came over with his dad. He was wearing a Braves cap and Braves shirt, kind of letting us know he was a Braves player.

Klesko and I shook hands with him. The next day was the clinic, and Andruw was there. We were taking batting practice, trying to put on a show like we were at a home run derby. That was the first time I saw Andruw take batting practice. For his size, he was hitting bombs. "Wow! He can hit!" I told myself.

We came back to Atlanta, and the 1995 season started. I kept hearing that kid's name—Andruw Jones…Andruw Jones…Andruw Jones. He was putting up big numbers. When I finally decided to see who this kid was, I saw the picture and said, "Oh, my God! It's that skinny kid from Curacao!"

I kept saying, "I knew he was going to do something!" because he was hitting those bombs when we were in Curacao. He was playing at Macon in Class A. I was blown away how well he was doing (25 home runs, 100 RBIs).

The following year, he started the season somewhere else (Durham to Greenville to Richmond), did even better, and he wound up in the big leagues at the end of the 1996 season—in August when he was only 19 years old. He didn't waste any time in the minor leagues. He came on really fast!

That was around the time when Paul Kinzer was becoming an agent. When we were in Curacao, he was talking a lot with Andruw's dad. He was working on becoming an agent, so he was trying to recruit him. But

Andruw's dad wanted to hear from other people, and he wound up with Scott Boras the next year.

So Andruw came up to the big leagues in 1996. His first at-bat was against Curt Schilling with the Phillies. Andruw fouled off a few pitches and wound up striking out. I said, "Welcome to the big leagues."

But it only took him a couple of games to adjust. He was only 19 years old, but he hit five home runs in 31 games. Unbelievable!

He only batted .217, but the Braves didn't care. Look at what he did in the World Series. He hit a home run in his first World Series at-bat at Yankee Stadium off Andy Pettitte, breaking Mickey Mantle's record as the youngest player to hit a World Series homer. And he hit another one his next time up—two home runs in his first game—becoming only the second player to do that.

When Andruw came up, he didn't really act cocky. He'd strike out and smile, and some people didn't like that. A lot of people would have liked to see him get angry, but he just laughed, walked back to the dugout, and put down his helmet. You never saw him throw anything. He wasn't cocky, though.

A lot of guys have to dress up in women's clothes their first year. It's rookie hazing. Just for the fun of it. Tradition. But I don't think Andruw ever did it, as far as I remember.

I remember I was supposed to wear these green women's shoes as part of my hazing, but they didn't fit me. I told the guys, "I'd be glad to wear the green shoes, but they're too small for me. I can't wear them." So I got out of it. They never came back for me.

Andruw never dressed up like the other rookies. He was a tough cookie. Normally every rookie had to do it when we flew to Montreal, because that's when you had to go through customs. You had to walk through the whole airport. People would see you. That was part of it.

We didn't go back that year, and the next year, they said, "Javy you didn't have to do it last year." I said, "Yes, I had to wear the green shoes." I lied, because I didn't want to do it. I got away with it!

You know what's happened to Andruw now? He hasn't gotten that second chance. He's getting contracts, but he hasn't had anyone willing to give him a starting position. You let him get 600 at-bats again, and he could come back and put up the numbers like he used to do.

The worst he would do is hit 15 or 20 home runs. Someone should give him that chance. The Rangers gave him a chance, but he was platooning.

With the White Sox, he'd hit home runs, and the next day he'd be on the bench. Same with the Yankees. If someone put him out there every day, they might see the old Andruw.

I NEVER HAD A REALLY CLOSE RELATIONSHIP WITH MARK WOHLERS. We did play together at Richmond. He came up to the big leagues, and it was hard to figure him out. *Is this guy sarcastic or serious or is he a jerk?* I wondered. You just didn't know. It was hard to figure him out.

When he had his control, his stuff was very, very tough. His fastball would just jump out of his hand. And then he had that splitter that he learned later that was just nasty. It was hard to catch, but the more I caught him, the more I learned how to catch that pitch.

A lot of times it looked like a knuckleball because it didn't rotate. It was hard to catch him. That's why a lot of times when he pitched the ninth inning, Bobby Cox pulled me out and put in Eddie Perez to catch. Eddie would be fresh coming out of the bullpen, and Wohlers can be wild. Even when he wasn't wild, he threw some pitches in the dirt to try to get the hitter to chase one.

When Wohlers was in control, he was one of the hardest pitchers to hit in my opinion. Yes, he never was quite the same after the Jim Leyritz home run in the eighth inning of Game 4 in the 1996 World Series. Eddie was catching when Leyritz hit the home run. Bobby pulled me out when he took out Mike Bielecki for Wohlers in the top of the eighth.

I don't remember Wohlers being out of control or throwing things or anything after the Leyritz home run He was frustrated, devastated, I'm sure. I was so mad and disappointed that we lost the game—not because of the Leyritz home run, but because we would have to go back to New York, and none of us wanted that to happen.

Don't get me wrong. New York is a really, really nice city. It's a nice city to visit—but not a nice city to play in. The fans are all over you. It is very tough.

Philly has the worst fans in baseball, but the Yankees—not the Mets—are next. Cubs fans can be really rude too. You see all these drunk kids in the outfield talking shit.

My wife was watching me play against the Cubs, and she was getting popcorn and other stuff thrown at her. Not just her, but the other players' wives too. The same thing happened in Philly—the fans throwing stuff at her. Boston can be bad, but just because they're right on top of you. They're not as nasty as Philly, New York, or Chicago.

WHEN I FIRST MET STEVE AVERY, I looked at him as a very important player in the organization. He was a No. 1 draft pick in 1988. All eyes were on him. He had really good stuff when he first came up.

I watched him throw in the bullpen in the minors, and I saw how hard he was throwing—breaking ball and everything. I was thinking, *I'm glad I don't have to face him.*

When I came up to the big leagues, I don't think Avery was happy to see me behind the plate when he pitched. I don't think I was his favorite catcher. I respect that. The one thing I would have loved for him to do was to talk to me and fix things instead of talking behind my back. Those are just rumors. Was it true or not? I don't even know and don't want to know now.

If he or anyone else had a problem, I was all ears and would have been glad to listen to them and talk about it. I started catching Avery a lot in 1994, the year I came up and started catching every day. He had a great year in 1993 (18–6) but was never the same after that. He might have pointed to me and said I was the reason for that. I don't know. I know he liked Greg Olson as a catcher.

But Avery lost his speed. I think it was mechanics. I don't know what happened to him, to be honest with you. He was doing well and then completely lost it. He was only 24 years old in 1994.

I don't think he was a big fan of Leo Mazzone's either. I saw Avery and Leo arguing on the mound and in the clubhouse quite a few times. They were very frustrated with each other.

What happened to Avery is a mystery. All I know is I was getting frustrated because I couldn't catch him and help him be the guy he had been earlier in his career. I felt bad because I wasn't any help to him.

From my standpoint, I wanted to see every pitcher I caught succeed. And I'd like for every pitcher to give me credit for that. I always did the best I could behind the plate for that reason—to help the pitchers succeed. There's nothing better in the world than to hear a compliment from your teammates about what a good job you did for them. Unfortunately, it didn't happen with Avery.

I GOT THE CHANCE TO HANG OUT WITH FRED MCGRIFF A LOT and get to know him better. He was like Galarraga—down to earth, a really nice person. Everybody liked Crime Dog. He was like a big teddy bear. I never saw him in an argument with anyone. He was a big-time Tampa Bay Buccaneers fan, very loyal to his city!

He and Mark Lemke were inseparable. It was fun to watch them and to be around them. Lemke was a funny guy, and McGriff could be funny when he wanted to be. He didn't say much, but he could be funny when he did. Tremendous guy, tremendous teammate, tremendous player.

I remember a joke we played on him once because he was terribly afraid of snakes. Charlie O'Brien brought this frozen rattlesnake to the clubhouse. Its mouth was open and the rattle was up like it was ready to strike. They put it in McGriff's chair, and his jersey was on top of it.

Everyone was sitting around, just waiting for him to get to his locker, and I remember he was in the shower and getting ready to get dressed. When he pulled up that jersey, he ran away screaming his lungs out. The Crime Dog nickname didn't fit him at that time. More like the Scaredy Dog! Or the Crying Dog. He was so scared. It's hard to describe his face or how he screamed. I'd never heard anything like it. You picture Crime Dog being a badass guy, but he wasn't that day.

I'm not sure why McGriff and Lemke were such good friends. Crime Dog liked people who made him laugh, and Lemke could always make him laugh. They were great guys. One time, Fred, Lemmer, and I were eating out. Every time Lemmer wanted to make a joke or make fun of someone, he would pull out his front two teeth. I forget how he got them knocked out in the first place.

Anyway, we were ordering at a restaurant, and I think he wanted to order fish or something. The waitress told him to order steak or pork or something else that was good and that she recommended.

Then he said, "Yeah, but I don't want to hurt my teeth," and he pulled out his teeth. "I don't have any teeth to chew with!" And he started laughing without his teeth.

Crime Dog and I were dying laughing! And if you heard Crime Dog laugh, it would make you laugh even more. He had the funniest laugh ever—except for Vinny Castilla. Anyone would tell you the same thing. I wish I had recorded it. He'd laugh on the bus, and everyone on the bus would be laughing just because of him.

Lemke and I went to Puerto Rico once to do an event for St. Jude Children's Hospital, a cocktail thing. We went to the event and then we played golf the following day.

The night we went to dinner, we saw this guy in the street, a homeless guy in a wheelchair, and he had a credit card machine. If people wanted to give him money and they didn't have change, they could swipe their card to give him money! And he had a website—a homeless guy! Only in Puerto Rico!

I told Lemke, "I gotta take a picture of this, because no one is ever going to believe it."

I took a picture, and when I got home, I used Photoshop to substitute Lemmer's face for that guy's face. It was pretty funny.

DURING SPRING TRAINING WHEN I WAS IN THE MINORS, I'd always go to the major league field in West Palm Beach to watch the players practice. I liked to see the major-leaguers practice their hitting and watch the pitchers throw in the bullpen, to see how hard they threw and why they were in the big leagues. I'd see pitchers throwing 90-plus miles per hour with big breaking balls, and I'd say, "That's why they're here."

Two of the pitchers I watched a lot in the bullpen were John Smoltz and Tom Glavine. Obviously, they were the talk of camp because they were so good. Back then it was Smoltz, Glavine, and Steve Avery. Everyone said how good they were.

When I first got a taste of the big leagues and started catching them, I was amazed that a year prior I had been in the minors and was watching them throw in the bullpen during spring training and now there I was catching them. I thought it would be hard, but it actually was a lot easier because of their control.

In the minors, a lot of pitchers have control problems, which is tough on catchers. It's something you constantly have to deal with. But when you get to the big leagues, everyone has good control. It was like going from driving a go-cart to driving a Cadillac!

I especially liked catching Smoltz, because he was what I called a "powerful" pitcher. He had really good stuff. When he'd strike guys out, it made me feel good, like I was contributing, because I was calling the pitches. His slider and split-finger were really nasty.

He usually threw what I called and was a lot of fun to catch. I also liked catching him because he threw hard and had a slide step, so it was easier for me to throw out guys at second base. He gave me more time. I wish all the pitchers had done that.

Glavine and Greg Maddux were slower to the plate, so it made it harder to throw guys out. I really liked to catch Maddux, even though I didn't get to do that very often. I liked to catch him because his games went fast. He didn't waste any time. It didn't matter how bad the situation was. I wasn't worried because he could get out of it so easily. That's why he was so good. I always felt we were going to win when he pitched.

Glavine always found a way to win too. He was a lot slower than Maddux and Smoltz. He really took his time and had a lot of 3–2 counts, but sometimes the hitters would get impatient and get themselves out. That was his plan, and he never changed it. His games lasted longer. He could pitch quick games if hitters were impatient, but it was either very quick or very long. There was no in-between.

Because he was a lefty, he could keep the runners close at first, but he was still slow to the plate. He developed a slide step later in his career.

I KNEW JOHN ROCKER WAS A HEAD CASE, but before he did that interview in *Sports Illustrated* in 1999, we got along. No problem at all. He got along with Randall Simon too. The three of us actually went out together one night in Tampa. We had an awesome time—friends, teammates.

After that interview, I tried to put myself in his shoes to understand exactly what he meant, whether it was in a bad way or if he was just joking around.

Regardless of what he said about how Randall looked, he knew Randall was a good guy, he liked him, and he liked to be around him. But he said things he shouldn't have said. He caused a big distraction for the team.

I do not think he's a racist. He went to Andruw Jones' wedding. He dates Dennis Martinez's daughter.

It was his anger talking. It wasn't the real Rocker. When he would get mad, he would completely lose his temper. You could tell it was somebody else taking over his body. I don't know what caused it, but the guy who took over his body definitely wasn't him. And when he was doing that *Sports Illustrated* interview, I think it was the second character who was talking.

Once he cools down, he's an awesome guy. We're still friends. I invited him to my tournament, but unfortunately he couldn't come. Even though he's a nutcase, he's a good guy, and a lot of people still like him. The HBO show *Eastbound & Down* was inspired by John Rocker.

NO MATTER WHEN YOU'RE READING THIS, Julio Franco is probably somewhere working out.

When he first came to the Braves in 2001, I was surprised he was still playing. He was 43 years old and hadn't played in the big leagues since 1997 (except one game with Tampa Bay in 1999). He'd been playing in Mexico and really hitting the ball.

When I first heard he was going to be with the Braves, I thought it was as a coach! But I always admired him when he was with Texas, and I thought, *This is a Latin guy I can learn from.*

Most of the time I was with the Braves, Eddie Perez and I were the only Latin guys. There were others who would come and go, but most years it was Eddie and me. I always wanted to have a veteran Latin player who could give me his views on what it takes to stay in the majors a long time, and Julio was perfect for that.

He and I talked a lot—mainly about baseball and how much you have to sacrifice in order to stay in the big leagues.

From everyone's perspective, he was a very good teammate, and he helped the Braves in a lot of ways, both psychologically and with his bat. He was unbelievable as a pinch-hitter. He really did his part for the Braves. Everyone liked him, and I know I learned a lot from him about baseball and about life. I know if I went to his house right now, he'd be working out, even though he's 53 and he's been retired since 2007.

EDDIE PEREZ IS QUITE A CHARACTER. I met him in 1988, my first year of pro ball. At the time, I had a second cousin playing in the Braves' farm system—Johnny Maldonado, who signed as a pitcher in 1987. He and Eddie played together that year, and when I signed, my cousin told me about Eddie and introduced us in spring training.

We didn't play on the same team together until 1991 at Durham. Before that, we'd always see each other in spring training and go our separate directions to different teams. But we became really good friends. We were together at Durham, Greenville, and Richmond, and he first came up to the big leagues a year after me, in 1995.

Eddie is a funny guy. He doesn't have the best physique in baseball, but he makes jokes about himself and cracks everyone up. He's also very scared of a lot of things. He knows people like to laugh at him being scared, and sometimes he might exaggerate things, but he's really scared! When Ned Yost was with the Braves, he was constantly scaring the crap out of Eddie. He loved watching Eddie get scared about something. It was so funny.

At the same time, he always knows about everything going on in the world, especially gossip. He could work on *The View*. He knows the latest on everyone and everything. If there's breaking news, Eddie knows it two days before.

We live near each other now, and we stay in touch. I'm the godfather to his son, Andres. His son can really hit the ball a long way, and he'll probably sign someday when he's older.

Of course, Eddie has a lot of baseball knowledge too. He's not just a bullpen coach; he's also a mentor. He wants to see players succeed, and he's been there and done everything in baseball, so he can tell the young guys what they need to know.

OTIS NIXON WAS SUCH A GREAT GUY. It was really something the way he and Eddie Perez joked around with each other about being "ugly." Every time Eddie would see Otis, he'd scream because he said he was so ugly…and every time Otis would see Eddie, he'd scream for the same reason. It was really hilarious. Everyone was always laughing at them and the comments they made to each other.

Otis was our gadget guy too. He used to own an electronics store, and probably 90 percent of the guys got their cells phones and other appliances from him.

He was very likeable. We still stay in touch and play in some golf tournaments together. He does a lot for the community.

I didn't get to know Deion Sanders well, but he always called me his "Latino brother." My first full year in Atlanta was 1994, and Deion got traded to Cincinnati that year in late May.

During spring training, we played the Mets in Port St. Lucie, and after the game, he and I took a limo to West Palm Beach to shoot a Powerade commercial. We did the commercial, and just when they were about to start airing it, Deion got traded. So they cut his image out of the ads and just used me!

The media was always all over him. I don't know how he put up with it. I would sit at my locker and listen to all the stupid questions the reporters asked him and just shake my head. I guess that was the price of fame he paid for playing baseball and football.

He and Otis Nixon were good friends, and they were always laughing at each other. He was always fun to be around.

I remember when he got traded, he gave me a black leather Mizuno bat bag. He said, "Here you go, my Latino brother!"

THE MADDUX FILE

THE BRAVES ALWAYS HAD A MEETING BEFORE THE FIRST GAME of every series. Pitching coach Leo Mazzone started it, and we went down the other team's roster player by player, mentioning each name and how we were going to pitch to them.

Then Leo might have a quick meeting with that day's pitcher, but I wasn't involved in that. I listened to his first meeting, and that's the plan I kept in mind.

I played with the Braves for most of my career, so I didn't know any other way of doing things. I thought what I was doing was the right thing. But when I went to the Orioles in 2004, they had a different approach. We'd have the meeting, and then the pitcher, the pitching coach, and I would have our own meeting. When I went to Boston in mid-2006, it was pretty much the same thing.

With Atlanta, Greg Maddux always called the starting catcher into the video room. Paul Bako, Henry Blanco, whoever. And whenever I caught him, we had a talk before the game. But Maddux was the only one who did that. Maddux would have the opposing batters cued up, and we'd say, "First hitter, this is how we're going to attack him. We'll start by throwing breaking balls and end up with a fastball in." We'd do the same thing with the second hitter, the third, and so on.

Then we'd break down different situations, such as, "If someone's on base and this guy is hitting, we're going to start this way."

We did it like that for every single player. Everyone has a different philosophy. I always wanted to stick with what we discussed in Leo's first meeting—what are each hitter's strengths and weaknesses. If someone's strength was middle-in, I didn't need to have a meeting with the pitcher, because I knew a pitch on the middle-in part of the plate was the last thing I was going to call against that hitter.

But hitters make adjustments, and then we have to adjust too. For example, the first two at-bats, we would stay away from that middle-in. But the third at-bat, the hitter knew he had to change, and it was my job to call a different area. I constantly had to switch.

As a catcher, it was my responsibility to make sure I had the hitter out of rhythm. Of course, it was impossible to call the perfect pitch.

But let's say I called a fastball, and the guy hit a home run. I needed to analyze the pitch I called before that pitch and how we got him out the at-bat before and how I would approach him the next time he came to bat. I needed to remember all that and analyze it. I had to make sure we switched the strategy with that hitter the next at-bat.

But when you can pitch the way Maddux pitched, when you have that kind of movement on the ball, you can tell the batter, "Sinker in," and he still can't hit it.

When you have Maddux's kind of ability, there's not much to talk about. I remember Sammy Sosa hitting one of the longest home runs off Maddux on a changeup. Righties hardly ever throw changeups to righties. They throw them to lefties. The changeup has a tendency to break down and away from lefties or down and in to righties. And down and in is what a power hitter is looking for.

So Maddux threw that changeup to Sosa and boom—home run, 500 feet!

It was nobody's fault. That was the plan. What that means is that the inning before he probably struck out on a similar pitch. But the following at-bat he was ready for it.

But it's hard for a pitcher to see what kind of adjustment the hitters make at the plate. I remembered how every hitter stood at the plate. Some players stayed close to the plate, and then the next at-bat, you'd see them moving back, looking for something in. If they were standing close and looking away, that's when you would attack them inside.

Sometimes the hitters set up inside so that the catcher thought they were looking for the outside pitch—but it's a trick. They were actually looking for the inside pitch, and then they would just step back and hit it. I saw all those kinds of tricks.

Vladimir Guerrero, for example, normally hit with his pinkie finger out. That was his approach. Anything away, he killed. We started pitching inside on him because he couldn't hit with his pinkie like that. He choked up a little bit, looking for something in. I knew what he was doing, so every time I saw him choking up and looking for something in, I'd call for a fastball or something away. If he had his pinkie out, I'd call for something inside. But sometimes, he changed his grip at the last second and brought his pinkie up on the handle. Those are the things pitchers don't know but catchers watch for.

It's a constant series of adjustments. That's why I was so confused when I went to Boston. The Red Sox have a million pages on each hitter, and there's a red square—a hot zone—for each player. I was trying to avoid that hot zone, but we were still getting raked.

They completely broke the routine I had with the Braves and Orioles. I had to go by their approach, with meetings that lasted longer than an hour, going through all these pages that I had to study. Maybe it worked for Jason Varitek, because he only played for Boston, and that's all he knew. But for me, I had a totally different plan, and it didn't work. It was a big change.

As a hitter, I didn't hit the fastball every day. Some days I'd rake the fastball, and some days I'd be hitting the breaking ball better. As a catcher, you need to know each hitter and which pitch to throw him on any particular night or during any particular at-bat. If a hitter doesn't hit the changeup his first two at-bats, then the third at-bat, you might start him with a changeup just to see if he's made an adjustment. If he gets a good hack at it, then you go with something else and maybe come back with the changeup later in the game.

Ned Yost and Pat Corrales were my two mentors. Because of them, I became the catcher I was. They both worked with me on my catching, and they did a great job. Ned worked with me on my catching skills, and Pat also worked with me on the attitude I needed to stay in the big leagues.

"You need to show the team your work habits," he said. "You need to show them you're trying to get better, that you're not just happy to be in the big leagues. Don't get to the clubhouse late, and don't leave early."

Little stuff like that shows the coaching staff and manager that you're interested in not just being a good baseball player but in getting better.

It's hard to get to the big leagues, but it's even harder to stay in the big leagues. Corrales helped me work on my attitude, work habits, and communication. This was mainly when I was a prospect in Double A and Triple A. He always took care of me in spring training.

When other people said, "He's not ready to be in the big leagues," he said, "He is ready." He also worked with me on how to handle the pitching staff and my catching skills.

Overall, in my opinion, I was a good receiving catcher. I couldn't give a better target to the pitcher. I couldn't position myself on the corner better.

I got in trouble with the umpires for being five inches away from home plate. I wasn't doing it for me. I was doing it for the pitcher so he could have a good game. I always liked to challenge the umpires. The Braves told me to set up outside. That was it. They didn't tell me to set up five inches outside. It was more me challenging the umpire. I'd just gradually sneak out there during the game.

Sometimes I'd set up outside and the umpire would call a ball. But I'd go back out there again. He might have missed that pitch, so I'd go back out there again to see if he had changed his mind. Sometimes I'd try it three, four times. Set up in the same position, and sometimes the umpire would start calling strikes.

I think they started putting in the catcher's box because of me. The whole league was complaining about the Braves pitchers getting the strike zone outside. When the box was there, I had to stay inside more.

One year I got in trouble with umpire Angel Hernandez because I was stepping outside the box. I had to tell him, "I'm 6'3". My feet have to be outside the box. My glove is inside the box, so concentrate on where the glove is." Being that tall might have helped expand the strike zone a little bit. I always tried to give a big target.

My glove actually was on the outside corner. If I'd had to get my feet inside the box, then the strike zone would have been between the outside corner and the middle of the plate. That's where my glove would have been. So my feet had to be outside the box in order for me to get the glove on the outside corner.

We had a big argument. Hernandez took his mask off in front of me. He was completely showing off.

He said, "You better get your feet inside that box. This is a warning!"

I said, "Do you really have to say it that way?"

Bobby came out. It was ridiculous. I don't remember if he got tossed or not—but he probably did!

So I'd set up inside and give the sign, and then I'd start moving my feet to get to the outside where my foot was outside the box.

In some ballparks, the box was wide, and in some it was narrow. The wide ones were perfect. I liked them.

But in Milwaukee, I said, "What's going on here?" It was ridiculously narrow. I'm sure some teams did it intentionally because the Braves were coming!

The Braves pitchers didn't have the fastest delivery to home plate, which affected my throwing. I would say 70 percent of the time, the runners stole the bases on the pitchers. A lot of times, I didn't even throw the ball because the guy got such a big jump.

The few runners I threw out at second base came when Smoltz was pitching. He had the slide step and a fast move to home plate, and he threw so hard. That allowed me to have time to throw to second base. I had a hard time with Glavine and a lot of the other pitchers we had.

I didn't have the best arm. I told myself the weights had a lot to do with it. I lifted so many weights during my career that it might have affected my elbow. I never suffered pain in my shoulder. It was more my elbow that bothered me. I didn't have the best arm, but it wasn't that bad either.

Before I stopped catching Maddux, the guy I didn't catch was Smoltz, basically because he had a pretty nasty split-finger that was hard for a catcher to block. And he was a little wild. He was the wildest guy in the pitching rotation.

They let Eddie or whoever was backing me up catch Smoltz most of the time. I caught Maddux in 1994. In 1995 Bobby decided that someone else would catch him. Some of the rumors were that Maddux had such a slow motion to home plate that runners got a big jump off him. Bobby wanted a fresh catcher with a fresh arm who had a better chance to throw out the runners.

Another rumor was that I didn't call a good enough game for Maddux and that when there was a man on second base, I took too long giving signs. I also heard that Maddux didn't need as much offense as the other pitchers. If he got one or two runs, that was enough to win a game. So they didn't need my bat in the lineup.

Regardless of the reason, I opted not to let it bother me. If he didn't come to me to tell me what I was doing wrong or that something I was doing bothered him, how was I supposed to fix it? I didn't want to approach him to ask him that question, because if he did have a problem with me and I asked him what it was, chances were he wasn't going to tell me. He'd just leave things the way they were. If he had a problem with me and didn't approach me, then he didn't want to resolve anything. And if he didn't have any interest in resolving it, then neither did I. Just left things the way they were.

After a while, I just didn't care what the reason was. I just took my day off and stayed ready, because most of the time he pitched, I wound up catching at some point in the game anyway.

A lot of people asked me, "Why don't you catch Maddux?" and I always gave the same answer: "Ask Bobby Cox, because I don't know."

It was Bobby who put me on the bench, not Maddux. If Bobby had wanted me in there, I'd have been catching every time Maddux pitched, whether he liked it or not.

At the same time, I asked myself, "What could be the reason?" He won a Cy Young Award in 1994, and I was catching him all the time. Charlie O'Brien was catching Smoltz, and I was catching Maddux. I caught 22 of his 25 starts that year. He even had a slightly better ERA that year (1.56) than he did in 1995 (1.63) when O'Brien caught most of his starts.

It seemed like everyone had a theory. Another rumor was that Maddux was racist. That can't be true, because Eddie was his "personal catcher" for a long time, and so was Henry Blanco. They're both Latin like me, so that can't be the reason.

Obviously I respected Maddux as a pitcher. He was one of the best ever. He always liked to speed up the game. When there was someone on second base, rather than me giving a bunch of signs and Maddux shaking me off, he already had a set of his own signs ready.

For example, if there was a man on second base, he would catch the ball in a certain way when I threw it back to him. I knew that the next pitch would be a fastball away. As soon as he threw that pitch, before I threw it back, he would touch his cap, and that meant the next pitch would be a curveball. He threw that pitch and then put his glove to his face when I threw it back. That meant changeup. Or if he put the glove somewhere else, it meant fastball in.

I think he did that with all his catchers. The catcher didn't know what he wanted to throw anyway, so rather than shake him off, Maddux gave the catcher the signs. It was all about speeding up the game. It was easy for me, because I liked to speed up the game too. Of course, if a catcher got traded, he'd change the signs.

When there wasn't a runner at second base, I gave him the signs the usual way. But he still did something to speed up the game. For instance, with no one on base, I might give him the sign for a fastball away, but he threw a changeup. He'd tell me that in advance, though—"Be aware that sometimes when you call a fastball, I might throw a changeup." He just didn't want to waste time shaking me off.

One time in spring training I got a broken finger because of that. It was a 3–2 count with a man on first base. There was a lefty hitter. I called a fastball away. With a 3–2 count, the runner was ready to go, and I was ready to throw him out. I got up a little early. But Maddux threw me a changeup on 3–2 instead of the fastball, so the ball hit me on the top of the glove and fractured my ring finger on my left hand. The guy was safe at second too! I missed two weeks of spring training because of that.

The times not catching Maddux really bothered me were when someone was pitching for the other team who I knew I could really hit! It also bothered me when the playoffs started and he was pitching the first game and I didn't start because of that. Obviously I wanted to be the starting catcher when the playoffs started. That happened in the 1995 World Series, too. Charlie O'Brien started the first game because Maddux was pitching. I wanted to be out there. It just bothered me a few times.

What really bothered me was when it was supposed to be my day off, but I wound up playing anyway. That happened about 85 percent of the time. Eddie would get a couple of at-bats, and then they'd take him out and put me in. It was hard for me to sit on the bench and try to enjoy a day off, knowing it was probably only temporary. It happened so many times that I knew I had to be ready. At the end of the game, I'd be in there.

If it was a close game, and it usually was, I felt bad if we lost, like it was my fault. Maybe I came in and struck out twice. It made me mad because it was supposed to be my off day.

For an off day, I would much rather have had Sundays off than not catching when Maddux pitched. That gave the backup catcher a chance to catch all the pitchers. With Eddie catching Maddux all the time, if I was out for a few days, then he had to catch Smoltz and Glavine, and he wasn't used to it. He was only catching one guy, so it was hard for him to be on the same page with the other starters. Plus, Sunday games are usually hot day games, so they take more out of you.

Maddux and I never talked like friends. We'd say hi to each other and goof around like you do in the clubhouse. But we never had a sit-down conversation. To be honest, that's the way it was with the whole pitching staff.

I came from a different country. I had a totally different culture than the pitchers. They were American. They all played golf, and I didn't at that time.

I felt more comfortable being around the Latin players, because we spoke the same language. It was as simple as that. It wasn't because I didn't want to be around the American guys. I just felt more comfortable talking with people who spoke Spanish. That's why I never got involved with the pitchers off the field.

The majority of the American guys I hung out with were rookies. When they came up, they were pretty intimidated to be around the veteran guys. They felt comfortable being around the Latin guys. We hung out and did things together. It was cool. Mark DeRosa, Marcus Giles, guys like that.

I didn't consider myself the best catcher, but I wasn't the worst catcher. I was a pretty decent catcher. I could throw people out, hustle, call a good game, and work hard. Maybe I didn't work as hard during the season as some, but in the off-season, I was a bull. I couldn't stop working out and getting myself ready for the next season.

Maybe because of the language barrier I didn't communicate with the pitchers as much as I wanted to. Maybe if I could go back and do it all over again, I'd communicate more with the pitchers before the game. But once the game started, I thought I did a pretty good job of catching and calling the game.

Some people said, "Anyone could catch that pitching staff." They were probably right. But they could say the same thing about Jason Varitek with the Red Sox and Jorge Posada with the Yankees. They also had pretty good pitching staffs too, and they were considered two of the top catchers.

Of course, I know the Maddux thing totally affected my reputation as a catcher. One time I decided to check out my defensive numbers and compare them with all these other catchers. Based on the numbers, I wasn't that bad of a catcher. I had the fewest errors and the fewest passed balls.

Posada and Varitek had more passed balls and errors than I did. So why was I such a bad catcher then?

Not catching Maddux could have been the big reason some people thought that way. Who knows? It definitely hurt my reputation.

But like I said, looking at the numbers, I was right there with the rest. Yes, toward the end of my career, my catching skills weren't the same. But that was all after I hurt my hand. And like anyone else, I was getting older and my skills were going downhill.

Prior to Baltimore, I don't think I got credit for being the catcher I was, and I'm not asking for it now.

11

TRANSITION

WHEN I WENT TO THE ORIOLES IN 2004, PEOPLE WERE MAD AT ME because I had "left the Braves."

Ask John Schuerholz why he didn't offer me a contract. He never said I left the team. He said, "We already have plans at catcher with Johnny Estrada." Nothing else.

I remember I was in San Diego when I got the call. He said, "Javy, this is John Schuerholz. How are you? I wanted to give you a call to thank you for all the years you've been with the Braves. We have other plans with Estrada. We're going to go with him."

I don't remember him saying anything like, "We can't afford you." I guess he didn't say anything like that. He said he had his plan with Estrada, and he was sticking with him.

It was short. He didn't even give me time to say, "No offer?" There was nothing. I was speechless. I didn't even know what to say.

He was clearly telling me, "We're not going to offer you anything. We had to give up Millwood, one of our main pitchers, to get Estrada, and we want to make sure we use him."

Basically, I think I said, "That's business. I totally understand." And that was it.

The year before I had a pretty bad year, my worst year with the Braves. I knew I had one more year, and I told myself, "If I don't have a good year, I'll definitely be gone." Then when I had that monster year in 2003, I thought at least I would get two more years or something. But apparently it didn't matter what I had done that year. I was gone.

I know they had to pay Greg Maddux a lot of money, but they were drawing 2.5 million fans a year. Are you telling me they didn't have the money?

It was sad. My dream was to end my career with the Braves, to play my whole career with the Braves, just like Jorge Posada is doing with the Yankees. Just like Jason Varitek with Boston. Just like Chipper Jones in Atlanta.

I was with Gina, and I told her what happened. I said, "I guess I'm not coming back with the Braves. That was John Schuerholz, and he said they're going to stick with Estrada for next year. So now let's see where I'm going to end up."

The only thing I didn't like is they didn't tell the fans, "Javy didn't come back because we can't afford him." Or, "We have a plan with Estrada." They never said anything. So the fans thought, *Oh, Javy. You left the Braves. Shame on you.*

I was like, "What are you saying? I didn't do anything. As a matter of fact, I played as hard as I could to get a two-year extension, and I got nothing. Zero."

It wasn't about money for me. I wanted to stay with the Braves. I would have taken a pay cut if I had to. But I didn't get any offer at all. I wish the Braves had done for me what the Yankees did for Posada and the Red Sox did for Varitek.

So that's one thing I didn't like about the whole thing. Schuerholz or someone should have made it clear to the media why I didn't come back to the Braves. It's not because I didn't want to. I wanted the fans to at least know that I wanted to come back.

That was the first time I'd experienced that situation. It's not a good feeling. First of all, I had everything in Atlanta. Suddenly I had to move. Just temporarily, but still I had to go somewhere else.

Where could I be happy? I was hoping San Diego would give me the opportunity to play there, just to be in California, with good weather, a new stadium, and I had the house there.

I did everything I could to play in San Diego, but they weren't going to pay either.

I talked to Padres manager Bruce Bochy when I saw him at a gas station. I told him, "I'd love to play with you guys." But Ramon Hernandez wound up there.

Age is what killed me. They could have had me. I was going to be 33 years old. He was only 27. He got two years for $7 million. That was why. He was there for two years, and then he went to Baltimore, where I was.

I hoped I'd get a call from the Dodgers. They were so focused on getting Vladimir Guerrero, who was a free agent. Ivan Rodriguez was a free agent too. Benji Molina was a free agent. And me. Nice year to be a free agent! I wound up getting three years for $22.5 million from Baltimore, and I really appreciate the confidence they showed in me.

So much of what a player gets in free agency depends on timing. There's no telling what the Braves are going to give Brian McCann when he's a free agent in a couple of years. If Joe Mauer is making close to $20 million…the Braves cannot afford that, but McCann doesn't want to leave the Braves. Maybe the Braves can come close to it but give him more years?

The Braves always get away with getting good players cheap. I'm surprised they gave Dan Uggla $62 million for five years. Where did that come from? That's what they paid Chipper. And compared to Uggla, Chipper put up better numbers in the past. Unbelievable. I was surprised how cheap they got Tim Hudson. The guy probably left $50 million on the street to play with the Braves in 2005. A pitcher like him could get $100 million for six or seven years. When the Braves traded him to Oakland, he was an awesome pitcher with Barry Zito and Mark Mulder. Hudson re-signed for four years and $47 million—almost $12 million a year. The Yankees would have signed him for $100 million, easy.

Based on my experience and the teams I played against, the places where I felt most comfortable were on the West Coast. Atlanta is an exception, of course.

Why the West Coast? One simple reason—weather. As a catcher, I wanted to be in weather where I could catch and perform best. Any city on the East Coast is so hot and steamy—or cold. It was hard on a catcher. Early in the season it's cold, then half the season is hot as hell. The time I felt comfortable catching was in May and sometimes September.

I'd have preferred any team in California, Colorado, or Arizona. I loved to play in any of those places because of the weather and also because the teams on the West Coast let you play. What I mean by that is they're not the Yankees or the Red Sox, where the media and fans attack you every time you make a mistake. They do some of that with the Dodgers too. I wanted to play where I could play comfortably—San Diego, Arizona, San Francisco, Oakland, even Seattle.

The less pressure I felt, the better I played—the better anybody plays. Some people like pressure, but I wasn't one of them. I played well with pressure, but if you gave me the choice to play with it or without it, I'd pick without.

Even in Atlanta when I had that bad year in 2002, people were saying things like, "Get Javy out of here. We need a new catcher." But all that criticism helped me get better that winter. I lost weight and prepared myself mentally. Losing weight was a big factor. Everybody knew I was going through a divorce at the time. That's pressure too.

It's not like I wanted to go to Baltimore, but it's not that I didn't like Baltimore.

When I signed with the Orioles on January 6, 2004, there were big expectations on me, Miguel Tejada, and Rafael Palmeiro. There was a big press conference when I signed. It was supposed to be a big year of change for the Orioles.

They changed everything. Palmeiro signed first on December 12, then Tejeda signed on December 18, and Sidney Ponson signed January 26.

We went to spring training with big expectations. When we got back to Baltimore, they had billboards with Tejeda, Palmeiro, and me on them.

We faced Boston in our first game. My first at-bat was against Pedro Martinez. My dad was there, Gina was there, and my aunt from Baltimore was there. The park was packed.

I kept watching Pedro. He liked to throw the first pitch for a strike. People were taking, taking, taking. I told myself, "I'm not going to take a pitch from Pedro, because once you fall behind in the count against him, you're done."

I was leading off the second inning, and there was no score. On the first pitch, he threw me a fastball right down the middle. I swung as hard as I could—home run! I couldn't have asked for a better start to the season. The place went nuts. I was already famous there after one at-bat!

I had three hits for the game, drove in three runs, and we won 7–2. It was a very, very exciting first game.

The first half of the season was great because we were playing good baseball. But then our pitching started to break down, and we couldn't keep up. We ended up in third place, 23 games behind the Yankees. We hit .281 as a team, which was third in the league, but we were ninth in runs allowed. If we scored 10 runs, the other team scored 11 or 12. We couldn't hold them.

But it was a pretty good season for me. It was frustrating being with Baltimore, though. It wasn't easy leaving the Braves, and I felt like I spent the whole year trying to get used to everything in a new city. Playing with the Braves for 12 years and then going to a totally new place with new people and playing for a new team wasn't easy.

And it was the American League. That was a change too. It was a transition. It was still baseball, but it took some time for me to accept that I was in a totally different place and I had to get used to it.

Actually, I don't think I ever got used to it. I really didn't like the American League at all. I liked the National League a lot better. The American League has a lot of great players, but what really makes it tougher is they have the DH. In the National League, you face the pitchers—they're quick outs. That's a big difference.

But the cities and ballparks in the National League are way better. Games in the National League are played a lot faster. Yes, the American League has a lot of competition. But as a catcher, you want the games to move faster. I was like, "Let me go rest my knees!"

After setting that home run record for catchers in 2003, I was trying to reach 300 home runs for my career. Unfortunately, in my second year with the Orioles, my season was cut short. I missed two months because of a broken hand from a foul tip.

I tried to come back that year—I don't know why they wanted me to do it—with six screws in my hand. But I wound up playing the rest of the season, even though we finished 21 games out of first place. The Orioles finished 74–88, in fourth place.

I still have those six screws in my hand. They decided to put in screws so I could get better in two months. That's what they told the doctor.

Could I get back? Yes. Pain free? No, I wasn't pain free.

It was very painful, especially throwing. When you throw, you kind of snap your hand, and that snap with all the screws in there didn't feel good. Fortunately, my hand doesn't hurt me now—unless I press on it really hard where there's a screw.

The injury happened on May 24, and I came back July 25. I was hitting .278 with seven home runs when I got hurt, and I finished at .278 with 15 homers.

I was very frustrated with the Orioles. The following year, I only played in 94 games combined, got 342 at-bats, and hit eight home runs. So I fell 40 home runs short of 300 for my career.

I never struck out 100 times in a season, but I only had 500 or more at-bats in 2004. If I'd had 500 at-bats regularly or even 550 to 600 like some guys, I'd hit a lot more home runs. In 2003, the year I hit 43, I had 457 at-bats. That was a home run every 10.6 at-bats, which was second in the majors to Barry Bonds. Catchers in the American League get more at-bats, but of course they can DH too.

I always tell people that if I could go back in time, I'd definitely try to play first base. It's not the same as catcher, but it's close, because you have to receive the throws from all the infielders and from the pitcher. It's the most active position in the field. I'd have had a lot more at-bats and probably played more years if I was a first baseman.

I hit 23 home runs my first year with the Orioles in 2004. That's the problem when you hit 43 home runs one year—people expect you to hit that many every year. I only hit 23, so everyone thought I was going downhill. The following year, I only hit 15, but I missed two months, and I played another two months after the surgery on my hand.

That winter, I prepared myself like I had before my big year in 2003. I wanted to come back healthy and have a monster year and extend my contract. Orioles manager Sam Perlozzo called me and asked, "How are you feeling?"

I said I was feeling good.

"Is your arm bothering you?" he asked.

I said, "No. Why?"

"We're here at the winter meetings, and we're all concerned about you," he said. "We're considering signing Ramon Hernandez to help you behind the plate."

I knew that if they signed him, he wasn't going to "help me behind the plate." He'd be the catcher every day.

Sam said, "What do you think about playing first base?"

And I said, "Sam, honestly, I'm preparing myself for the coming year, the last year of my contract. I don't want to experience a new position in the last year of my contract. I think you're picking the wrong time for me to start learning a new position. I've never played first base before. It's going to be a new start for me.

"The only way I can play first base is if I get an extension from the Orioles. If I can do that, I can totally start playing first base. But if I'm not going to get an extension, then I'd love for you guys to try to find me another team. I really need to catch and want to catch this year. I can't play first base, and I hate DH. I did it a few times, and it's not fun."

He said, "Okay. Sure enough," and hung up.

So they signed Ramon Hernandez. I found out the next day. And I never got a call from them. A week later, I called them. I said, "I see you signed Ramon Hernandez, and I haven't heard anything from you. What's the plan for me? What's my new role? What's going to happen to me?"

Perlozzo couldn't answer. He actually told me to call the general manager, Mike Flanagan. So I called Flanagan and left a message. He called me back and said, "Javy, me and [co-GM] Jim Beattie are going to be in Atlanta the day after tomorrow, and we'd like to have a word with you."

I said, "Sure. I'd like to talk about this situation."

So they came to Atlanta two days later. My wife and I met them at The Tavern over by Phipps Plaza. We sat and talked about all kind of things—except what we needed to talk about. Right at the end of our meal, I told them, "I'm working hard and want to extend my career. I want to extend my contract."

They just listened. They didn't say a word. I told them everything I wanted, and they just listened. They never said yes or no to anything. They just listened.

When the meeting was over, I felt like it had been a waste of time. A couple of days later, I called my agent and said, "I had this meeting with Flanagan and his assistant, and I want to know what's going on. Right now, I have no place on that team. I want to catch every day and put up some good numbers. I want to be able to extend my contract."

He called me back later and said, "They're willing to give you one year, an extra year, and it is for $3 million."

I said, "Wow…I'm not more valuable than that to this team?"

Anyway, I didn't accept the extension. Obviously, if I had known things were going to turn out the way they did, I would have made a different decision. They stuck with that price, so I asked them to trade me before the season started. But nothing happened. I was getting desperate. Spring training was around the corner, and I was not going to be the catcher. What was going to happen? I was freaking out.

Spring training started, and there was still no trade. It was like any other spring training. I was working out, but I didn't know what to do the first day. Catcher, first baseman, outfielder? Where was I going to go?

Every day I had to ask the coaches, "Where am I going?" I asked coach Rick Dempsey the first day, and he said, "You come back here with the catchers."

And I said, "Okay. I'll catch."

I caught bullpen the first day. I caught bullpen the second day. I said, "Okay, that's back-to-back days catching bullpen. Obviously, Ramon is going to be the starting catcher."

They told me I was going to play first base, but I hadn't even caught a ground ball yet. Nobody approached me to start working with me at first base. What happened?

So I talked to Perlozzo. "It's been a week, and I haven't done anything but catch bullpen," I said. "You told me in the winter that I'd be playing first base. I'd catch and play first base. Nobody has approached me about playing first base. I want to know what's happening. What's going on? Where do I fit in? What's my role?"

He said, "Well, this guy's supposed to work with you. I'll let him know tomorrow."

That was bullcrap. He knew no one was working with me. Anyway, the next day, he had one of their coaches start teaching me the basics of first base. Mainly he was hitting ground balls to me.

A couple of days later, I said, "I'm getting a lot of ground balls, but where's the guy telling me how to field, how to do things?"

They finally put a coach next to me telling me how to do things. I was already very frustrated.

I stopped catching bullpen so I could practice in the infield. So I wasn't catching at all. I was getting nothing but ground balls.

Then the World Classic started. I wasn't going to play for Puerto Rico, but that stirred up some controversy. Everyone wanted to know, "How can you not play for Puerto Rico?"

I told them I couldn't because I was learning a new position.

They said, "We'll take care of you. Come play for us."

So I went to Jupiter to practice with the Puerto Rican team, and Jose Oquendo (former major league infielder and manager of the Puerto Rican team) and Ivan DeJesus (former major league shortstop) worked with me like you wouldn't believe. In the few days I spent with them, I learned more than I had the whole spring training with the Orioles, because they were on top of me, teaching me how to field. I learned a lot.

I played in the World Classic, and then the regular spring training games began. Kevin Millar was playing first base for the Orioles. I came back to spring training from the World Classic and suddenly I was the DH! Millar was the starting first baseman. They'd already announced it.

In their mind, I know they thought all along I was going to be their DH. But I hated being the DH! All those years catching, I was a part of every pitch, involved in every single situation. All of the sudden, I had to DH. So, I was the DH, and a few times they put me at first base. I was only in one spring-training game behind the plate—the next-to-last game of spring training.

I couldn't get into any rhythm behind the plate, and I had very little practice at first base. The only real practice I had was in the World Classic. I had no position. I was frustrated from day one. You can tell by my numbers that I wasn't happy at all in 2006.

Unfortunately I carried all that frustration with me throughout the season. I felt like I was sitting on my hands on the bench. I didn't have any motivation to cheer for my team—that was very bad; that's wasn't me. I didn't care about the team. I didn't care about winning or losing.

I did care about hitting well. I was being selfish, but at the same time, I wasn't happy. I was frustrated. I was counting the days hoping the Orioles were going to trade me.

One day, pitcher Rodrigo Lopez decided to "hire" me as his personal catcher after he had about seven starts in a row. I caught him one game on May 25, and he won it. That made him 2–7. I became his catcher, and he started winning games. That's the only time I caught—when Lopez pitched. I think I started 19 games at catcher, probably all with him starting.

The frustration and not caring about anything…I felt so bad, because I knew that wasn't me. That wasn't the type of player I was, and it's not the type of person I was.

I cared about my teammates, but I didn't care about wearing the Orioles uniform.

There was a point where I didn't even play. I wasn't hitting, so I didn't play, and that made it even worse. Do you think I wanted to be there cheering for my team when we were way out of first place already?

There were days when I left in the ninth inning, before the game was even over. That's something I'd never done in my life, something I wasn't proud of doing. But, at the same time, I just didn't care. I felt like they treated me badly, so I wanted to treat them badly too. At some point, you just want them to ship you out.

It didn't happen at the trading deadline, but finally, in August, Jason Varitek hurt his knee. The Red Sox called the Orioles, and they decided to trade me August 4 for a player to be named later, which turned out to be outfielder Adam Stern.

I didn't want to go to Boston. I really wanted to get traded at the beginning of the season, in April or May, so I could still have most of the season to play.

I only caught one game in spring training and only started 19 games at catcher for the Orioles, so I wasn't ready to catch for Boston. My arm wasn't in throwing shape. My legs were stiff because I had only caught about once a week. I was out of sorts behind the plate.

Boston wanted me to catch every day, but I wasn't prepared— mentally or physically—especially in a big city like that. I'd have liked to have called my agent and said, "Can't you get me out of this?" But then everyone was saying, "This is the opportunity you've been looking for, to get out of Baltimore."

That was true, but the timing couldn't have been worse. It was too late in the year. Four months too late. Going to Boston, I had such a bad feeling because I wasn't prepared. Emotionally, I wasn't into the game. I was frustrated.

To try to get to know the whole pitching staff at that point was a real challenge. That's what spring training is for—to get ready mentally and physically and to get on the same page with all the pitchers.

The first time I caught for the Red Sox, I caught Curt Schilling. I'd faced him before, but I'd never caught him, so I didn't know what to expect. I did okay catching him. I wanted to impress them with my hitting. I wasn't thinking about getting a hit—I was thinking about hitting the ball out of the ballpark. It was hard, very hard.

At that time, I had my kids with me in Baltimore when they traded me. Gina had to stay in Baltimore. I had to take the kids with me. I called my dad in Puerto Rico to fly to Tampa Bay so he could watch the kids. That was another distraction.

I had to charter a private jet to take the kids with me. We got there and waited for my dad. I gave him the kids and said, "I'll see you at the ballpark."

It was uncomfortable. I was not in a good frame of mind—I had a new team, I had my family with me. I felt so out of place that I wanted to quit right there.

I didn't want to play, because in the back of my head, I knew I wasn't going to perform up to my standards. After all the frustration I'd been through that season, I just knew I wasn't going to perform. But, of course, there was nothing I could do but stay there and do my best.

When I joined the Red Sox in Tampa Bay, the team already was on a five-game losing streak. They were already going downhill. I started catching. We won the first game, but then we started losing. Then all the media started pointing at me. I was like, "What's going on here?"

The media always has to have something to talk about. Varitek was hurt, and they expected me to be as good or better than he was, but I hadn't been doing much of anything all season.

I already had a bad feeling about going there, I had a frustrating season with the Orioles, and now I had to listen to the media bash me. It made it even worse. Plus, I was getting booed every time I went to bat. All the fans were frustrated, not only with me but because the whole team wasn't winning.

So I went to manager Terry Francona's office and sat down and explained my situation.

I said, "I'm hearing all sorts of rumors. I don't know what to believe, but I want to be honest with you. I don't know how the pitchers feel with me behind the plate. I don't want to make anyone look bad. I want the best for the team. I want you to know if you don't want to catch me, if you want to use Doug Mirabelli, you won't hurt my feelings. He's been here a while and knows the pitchers a lot better than I do."

Francona said, "Don't listen to what those assholes say. You're doing fine. Unfortunately, the team isn't doing well, and they have to point at somebody. Don't let that bother you."

I said, "I know. I've never had to deal with that many people in the media. I just want to let you know I'll do the best I can, but if you don't want to play me, I understand."

After that, I played a couple of times, but I might as well have stayed on the bench the way things were going. Boston finished in third place with an 86–76 record, 11 games back, after finishing tied for first the year before and being the wild card.

Varitek got better, and I got a call from Francona one morning. He said he wanted to see me, and I told Gina, "Yes! I think I'm going to get released."

I felt so happy when I got there, and he said, "We're going to let you go. Varitek got better, and we respect you and don't like having a guy like you sitting on the bench. Thank you for everything."

I said, "I completely understand. I really appreciate it. Thank you for the opportunity. The way this has been for me, this is probably what I need. Thank you."

I left his office and felt so happy, and relieved. I went back to the hotel and hugged Gina and said, "This year is over."

But then I had to face the consequences. The reality was that nobody wanted me. My agent told me, "I know it was a year of frustration, but now we have to face reality. We're going to have a hard time finding a team that wants you."

I told him I understood. There was nothing I could do but get back into training, do the best I could, and see what happened. So that winter, I trained like normal.

Then my agent called and told me I had two choices. Two teams were interested in me—Kansas City and Colorado. Colorado wasn't very sure about their rookie prospect, Chris Iannetta. They wanted to know about my catching skills because I had hardly caught at all in 2006. I was leaning more toward Colorado than Kansas City.

I said, "I'm up for it. I'll do whatever they want me to do."

Colorado sent me to San Luis Obispo, California, to work with Jerry Weinstein, a catching instructor at Cal Poly–San Luis Obispo. He'd been a college coach, worked with Olympic teams, and worked in the Dodgers organization.

I flew to California at my own expense. They didn't pay me for anything. I started working with Weinstein, who was a tremendous instructor. He was one of those guys who did everything differently from any other instructor I'd worked with. He had videos. I loved it. I loved the way he trained catchers. Tremendous guy.

I was there for a week working with him and taking batting practice. My arm was almost ready. Things were going good, and he even told Colorado that I looked pretty good. But after a week, he took me to a speed and agility program in Santa Barbara. I started working out with that group, doing nothing but speed and agility for an hour and a half. Everything was good. Then the last few exercises, they had me do squats…but rather than go down and then come up, they wanted me to go up and down as fast as I could. I'd never done that before, but they wanted me to be explosive.

So, holding the weights, I did it once, and it was okay. Up and down… then what happened?

I hurt my back. I completely snapped my back. On the way back to San Luis Obispo, Jerry took me to a chiropractor. They cracked it and did everything they could, but for me, it made it worse. I was in pain. I called Jerry that night and told him, "I hope what we've done so far is good enough for you to give me a good recommendation, because I honestly can't do anything else."

My back was in pain, big time, so I had to leave. I had to drive from San Luis Obispo to Los Angeles to catch a plane back to Atlanta. It's about a three-hour drive, and with my back hurting, it was torture. I'd never had any back trouble like that before.

But Jerry gave Colorado a pretty good report. I don't know if Colorado signed me because they really needed me, or if they signed me because of my effort to go out there and work with Jerry. But they signed me. My back got better in about two weeks, and I pretty much kept doing what Jerry had taught me.

I was happy. I went to Tucson, Arizona, and started working with them. My arm wasn't the same after missing most of a full year of catching. It's not the same when you're not throwing every day, working on throwing to second base every day. And there were two weeks when I couldn't do anything while my back was getting better.

Anyway, spring training started. I was doing pretty well. The games started, and I was catching fine—blocking everything—and really starting to hit the ball. But I couldn't throw people out. It was just spring training, and it takes a while to get loose, but my throw wasn't there yet. My mechanics and everything felt good, though. My arm was strong.

Iannetta, the rookie, happened to have a pretty good spring training too. Based on how he looked, they decided to release me rather than send me to Triple A. I was 36 years old, so they weren't going to send me to Triple A. Unfortunately, when they released me, it was already halfway through spring training. It was pretty late to find another team. Most teams were pretty well set.

I waited a week to see if my agent could find another team for me, but after a week, he didn't find anything. So I decided not to play that year.

It was frustrating, because I felt I was having a good spring training. I was looking forward to playing in Colorado. I could already see myself being Comeback Player of the Year. That's how good I felt.

I love Colorado—the city of Denver, the weather, everything about it. So when they released me, I was heartbroken.

I told me agent I was shutting it down for that year. I was thinking about retiring, but I said, "No. Just take a year off and then start fresh." If the problem was my throwing, then I'd work on that all year. I probably focused too much on my arm. I worked out the whole year at the gym.

Then in November 2007, I called Chino Cadahia, a coach with the Braves (now with Kansas City). I wasn't expecting to come back and play in Atlanta. I just wanted to work out with him on my throwing. That way, whoever wanted me, my throwing would be there.

Chino is a tremendous catching instructor. He has his own philosophy, and I respect that. But when you ask a guy like me, someone who has been in the big leagues for 15 years, to change some of his mechanics, it's not easy. Maybe if I was starting as a rookie, then that would have been perfect.

If Chino had tried to work with my mechanics rather than changing my mechanics completely, that would have worked better for me.

We worked together in Peachtree City. I'd drive from Suwanee to Peachtree City—an hour and a half, every single day.

Before he was Bobby Cox's bench coach, Chino was a roving instructor in the minors for the Braves for many years. He was always at spring training. He'd throw me BP. I'd known him for a while. He helped Ivan Rodriguez as a catching instructor when he was in Texas.

So we worked together, and my arm felt great. My speed, my arm, everything was good. There were days when it was like 15 degrees, and I was there throwing to second base. We were filming everything.

And then he started talking to the Braves: "I'm training Javy, and he's looking pretty good. We'd like you to watch him throw."

Braves general manager Frank Wren came and watched me throw a few times, and at that time I decided to sign with a different agent. It was a little too late, but I went with Paul Kinzer. So, while I was working out with Chino, Kinzer called me and said, "The Braves offered you a minor league contract."

I said, "Awesome," and I told everybody. Everyone was happy.

Then after I signed, rather than working out in Peachtree City, I began working out at Turner Field every day with Chino. I already knew Braves starting catcher Brian McCann, and we started joking around. He wasn't living in the subdivision where I live yet, but he was looking at it. I saw him there several times visiting former Brave Mark DeRosa. Everything was good.

My trainer at the gym was super happy because all the training we did for a year had paid off. When spring training started, it was like I had gone into a time machine. I felt like I was back home. I'd never been happier.

But then I told myself, "This isn't your place yet. You're not on the team yet."

I kept that in the back of my mind. It wasn't a good feeling, because before when I was with the Braves, I'd go to spring training to get myself ready. That's all. I wasn't trying to make the team. I was already on it.

This time I had to do both—prepare myself and try to make the team. In order to make the team, I had to try to improve and impress the coaches. Hit home runs, block, and throw people out, because that's what people wanted to see if I could do—throw people out.

Unfortunately I had been throwing so much in the off-season that when spring training started, my arm was kind of tired from all that throwing. I threw so much with Chino that to make sure I felt good for spring training, I used ice on my arm every day. Even though it didn't hurt, it felt tight, so I used ice every day.

Spring-training games started, and I hit a home run in my first at-bat with the Braves. I was like, "Wow!" I felt even better.

But then the next time I played, it was a little different. I wanted to hit another one to impress even more. It didn't happen. I was catching well, blocking everything, and calling good games. A couple of guys tried to steal. I bounced one throw and threw the other into center field.

The one time I could have thrown the guy out, no one covered second base! Rafael Furcal was the runner, Kelly Johnson was playing second base, and Yunel Escobar was at shortstop. The ball was right there, and I was like, "Shit!" At least I felt good throwing it.

My hitting wasn't that good. I didn't have my timing down. Halfway through spring training, the Braves started making cuts. I think I was in the third cut. Eddie Perez called me into Bobby's office, and Eddie and Chino were there. They told me Corky Miller was the backup catcher the previous year and was going to be the backup catcher again.

Bobby said, "We think your hitting needs to improve. Your catching is good. Your arm needs to get better. We have a place for you in Triple A. You can work at first base and you can catch."

He was just giving me the choice. The problem was they had Clint Sammons as the starting catcher at Triple A. I stood there...thinking, thinking, thinking...trying to assess the whole situation.

First base? I had tried that with the Orioles, and it didn't work out. Catching was the only position I ever felt comfortable playing, and if I was going to be a backup, I wasn't going to be playing at Triple A. It sounded like the bench.

I said, "Bobby, thank you so much for the offer, but after what happened to me the last two years and what's happening now, I guess it's time for me to hang up the glove, because I'm not going back to Triple A. I don't think I deserve to be a backup at Triple A. So rather than embarrass myself, I'm going to quit. I'm going to retire."

Bobby said, "I understand. I respect your decision. Thank you so much."

He stood up, gave me a hug, and said, "Thank you for all the memories."

Eddie gave me a hug, and I left. It was very painful for me. It wasn't an easy decision after all those years. I'd put a lot of work into trying to come back. The whole year, I was working out while everyone else was playing.

I was about to cry. I told myself to hold it back, and I called my wife from the parking lot. I said, "They cut me. They wanted to send me down, but I would be a backup catcher at Triple A."

Their minor league team was Richmond at the time. If it had been Gwinnett then, like it is now, maybe I'd have felt differently. Gina cried, because she knew how much I had worked to try to make it, and it didn't happen. It was a very, very tough decision.

I knew once I said I was done, that it was over. I wasn't going to return. That was my comeback. That's why in 2007, I never officially said I was retiring. I took the year off with every intention of trying to come back the next year.

I was always looking for that second chance. I saw a lot of players get second chances, and Atlanta was known for giving a lot of players a second chance. Brian Jordan, Tom Glavine, Otis Nixon, Terry Pendleton…a lot of people. A lot of guys who left came back later. I was hoping I would have the same chance.

A lot of fans were cheering for me, pulling for me in spring training. I was hoping that would help my chances too. That didn't help.

I called my dad and let him know. He thought I could still play and that I should go find somebody else.

"Fire your agent!" he said.

I knew it wasn't the agent.

Then he said, "You should go to the minor leagues."

I said, "Maybe I should, but I'm proud. I don't want to put myself in a situation like that as a backup catcher in Triple A. I have pride."

The only place I could be a backup was in the big leagues. It was embarrassing for me. I couldn't see myself being in the bullpen at Triple A and warming up pitchers. If that was the case, I'd be in the dugout doing nothing, being lazy.

So the opportunity I was looking for never came. I never got the second chance to make a comeback. Look at Ivan Rodriguez, now with Washington. He's got a chance at 3,000 hits. But four years ago, he wasn't looking so good, and I thought he might not find a team until Houston signed him. Look at what he did with Houston. He actually got *three* chances. Washington decided to sign him and made him the starting catcher. I said, "God bless you, Ivan." That was exactly what I was looking for, but I never got it.

I knew if I got the chance to catch every day I'd prove that I was back. Physically, I was better than ever. But it didn't happen.

My dad said, "Why don't you go to Mexico and play there?"

I was frustrated. My dream was dead. I wasn't going to go to Mexico. I decided to retire and leave good memories for the fans rather than keep trying to make it and getting released by teams. I didn't want that.

I almost tried it in 2009, though. I told my agent to check and see if there was any interest. But I told him a lie. I said I was ready. But no one wanted me. I said, "Don't worry. I was joking."

12

AFTER BASEBALL

AT THE END OF 2008 I STARTED A BASEBALL BAT COMPANY. I began thinking about the business when I got released by Colorado in 2007. That forced me to ask myself, "What am I going to do now?"

Of all the ideas I had, I decided on a bat company. That idea came after I saw Omar Vizquel's baseball bat line, called Route 66. I thought it was a terrible bat. So I thought I would create my own bat and make it better.

I mention Vizquel because he was the first player I knew who was involved in a company selling bats to major leaguers. Royals Hall of Famer George Brett and Dodgers manager and former Yankees star Don Mattingly sold bats but not to major leaguers.

When I got released, I thought about starting a baseball academy or being a personal instructor or opening a batting cage, but I also had the baseball bat idea.

I decided to think about it, and at the same time, I started making sketches of what I wanted the logo to be. I was riding motorcycles and was fascinated with skulls, so I decided to use something with a skull.

I had quite a few logos that I wanted to give to a professional graphic artist to design the final logo. Once I had different options, I took it to a guy who has a tattoo parlor. He came up with the skull I have now. I didn't envision it without a chin, but that's the way he drew it, and I thought it was cool and different. And the head looks like a baseball with stitches. I stuck with it.

I named the company Bones Bat. Gina gave me the idea for the name Bones. The *B* is made of a *J* for *Javy* and an *8* because that was my number. You can see it at bonesbats.com.

They're good bats. If I had been playing, I would have used them. They're solid.

The reason I used *Bones* instead of *Javy* on the bats is because Brett and Mattingly used their names on their bats. I don't see that selling in the big leagues, because players don't want to buy a bat that has another player's name on it. It's an ego thing. To avoid that, I used the name Bones. That way it doesn't sound like it's Javy Lopez's bat.

I didn't have a sales representative the first year. I pretty much embarrassed myself by going to some teams and introducing the bats myself to players. I know players were looking at the bats and thinking, *Javy Lopez—playing baseball last year and now selling bats?* It was embarrassing, but I couldn't think of any other way to promote it.

After visiting a few teams, I decided that was it. There are people out there who do that for a living, and they're good at it. I wasn't good at it. I wasn't getting any sales, only a few, thanks to Paul Kinzer. He was an agent and was buying bats from me for some of his clients.

And the Braves helped me out too. They bought a few dozen for the minor leagues. That helped.

I gave away a lot of bats to a lot of major league players. How many called back to order a dozen or a half dozen? Zero.

I thought no one in professional baseball was going to buy bats from me. I figured my sales were going to come from Little Leagues, high schools, and at amateur tournaments—not from professional players. The next year I paid $16,000 to get a license from Major League Baseball, and I didn't get anything out of it. Most of the sales were to the minor leagues, and I was discounting the price a lot.

The third year, I decided not to renew the MLB licensing, because it wasn't working. Most of my sales were coming from dealers, retailers, online customers, and at tournaments I do every year. Hopefully it will get better. At least I don't have that big licensing fee.

My goal with this company is just to break even with what I've put into it so far. Once I break even, I want to keep doing it because it keeps me busy. Right now I just hope to recover all the expenses I've put into it. Hopefully I can do that in two more years.

I basically buy the same wood that all the good bat companies use. The wood is graded *A*, *B*, and *C*, and I buy nothing but grade *A*. It costs more, but I know what I'm buying is good quality wood. No matter who I sell a bat to, even if it's a nine-year-old who uses a 28-inch bat, he knows he's getting the same quality bat anyone in the big leagues is using.

Of course, it's wood, and it will break like any wooden bat if you hit it in the wrong spot. The difference is that when you hit it on the barrel, the ball is going to jump. I sell bats made of ash, birch, and maple. Birch and maple have been my biggest sellers.

I wish ash would do better, because that's what I used during my career. It's a really good wood, as long as you get a wide grain on it. Of course, it's hard to buy a pallet of 366 billets with nothing but wide grain on it. You can't do that. But when it comes to maple and birch, every billet is pretty much the same.

My other goal is to continue this company and later, hopefully, start selling apparel and maybe eventually aluminum bats and other baseball equipment.

I think Bones is a good brand. It's challenging administratively, but it can be manageable, and I think we can make more products later on.

SOMETHING ELSE I'VE DONE SINCE RETIRING FROM BASEBALL is take part in a program called Leadership Gwinnett. It's run by the Gwinnett Chamber of Commerce. Gwinnett is the county where I live, just north of Atlanta. It's where the Braves have their Triple A team now.

Leadership Gwinnett is a nine-month program of training and development that gives you a look at how the government works, and you learn about the education system, public safety, all sorts of things.

You learn how everything works in local government. One day it's education, and you learn how to run a school. Maybe you serve as a principal for a day, which I did at a local high school.

You learn how much work all these people do every day in order to run a school. You learn from them, and they hope that they'll get ideas from you that they can use in doing their jobs.

Another day was public safety. You're with the police force all day, and you see what they have to go through. After that, you look at a police officer in a totally different way. We should thank them every day for what they do, because they put their lives on the line to protect us every day. You go to their office, and you get to see how they train to become police.

Another day, they put us with the environmental department and you see how they keep the parks, the trees, and the rivers clean. You learn about the water-treatment system.

When you finish the program, they ask you for ideas. You have to talk about what you've learned in each section and tell them about any ideas you have.

Each week we'd talk about how to make things better in Gwinnett. It was very educational. There were three principals in the program when I was there, two mayors, lawyers. You get to meet all these people and create a good network.

They asked me to give a motivational speech. I said I'd never done that—at least not in English. I might have done it in Spanish, which is a lot easier for me, but in English it was something I'd have to work on. So I hired a woman to teach me how to be a motivational speaker, how to start, how to finish, and how to develop the content. I was getting very prepared, and then they changed the date, and I couldn't do it.

I would have been talking to people who didn't know anything about baseball. It's different if I'm talking to people about baseball. It was difficult to say I'd do it, and it also was a big relief when they changed the date!

But I told them if they wanted me to do it any other time, I would be glad to do it if I hadn't committed to anything else.

I played with a lot of Spanish-speaking players who were never afraid to just talk. If they made mistakes, they didn't care. They actually sounded funny.

Ozzie Guillen, now the Florida Marlins manager, is a good example. How funny does he sound when he speaks English? But he doesn't care. It is what it is. Take it or leave it.

There were quite a few players I played with who were just like him. They just said, "English is not my first language."

It's not mine either, but I continue to try to learn it, and Gina has helped me a lot. My older sons, Javy and Kelvin, don't speak much Spanish. But I talk to Brody in Spanish all the time.

Gina doesn't want me to talk to him in English. She says, "I'll talk to him in English, and you take care of the Spanish."

So that's what we do. I speak Spanish to him as much as I can. He's got books in Spanish and English. He watches the baby channel, and sometimes he watches *Dora the Explorer* so he can learn Spanish. I want to make sure he's bilingual, because that's always a plus.

Javy and Kelvin come to our house. I have them for five days, and my ex has them for nine. Javy Jr. is almost 6'0", and my 11-year-old—Kelvin—is pretty big too. Kelvin is playing baseball. Javy took a break from playing, but now he's practicing for next year.

I told him he better be practicing, because after missing a year, it will be harder for him to try to make the team. He needs to practice all year round if he wants to make it. Even then, practicing is not the same as playing real games.

He mainly plays first base and some outfield. He runs pretty well. He just needs to work on his defense. He's not the best hitter, but he's not the worst. He's a clutch hitter and a good contact hitter. He hits the ball hard.

Kelvin...that kid is killing me. I don't know if baseball is really his thing. He doesn't seem to care. He just plays the game and doesn't care if he's 4-for-4 or 0-for-4. He's still the same. He's not the best hitter, and he's not the worst either. He plays outfield and some third base.

They've both been playing since they were four years old. Maybe I burned them out?

Brody is going to start playing sports early, but I'm not going to put him in sports year-round. I want him to be a kid. I don't want him to be going from baseball to basketball to soccer all the time. If he plays baseball, that's fine, but in the winter, I want him to just be a kid and play with his friends.

I don't go to Braves games very often, maybe a couple of times per year. In 2010 I went to Opening Day. It started at 4:00 PM, and I left the house at 1:30. I got there at 5:00. It took me three and a half hours to get to the ballpark!

It's only a 45-minute drive, but it took three and a half hours to get to my seat and watch the game, just because of traffic. I got downtown in 40 minutes. The rest of the way—I couldn't move. I was right outside the stadium when Jason Heyward hit that home run in his first at-bat. I just heard the crowd. I said, "What happened?"

I DON'T HAVE MY OWN CHARITABLE FOUNDATION, but I help a lot of other people with their foundations. I've been helping Brian Jordan, Tim Hudson, and others. I try to help them the best I can by playing in their golf tournaments and donating my time.

In 2010 I started my own golf tournament to raise money for St. Jude Children's Hospital. It's called the Javy Lopez Celebrity Golf Tournament, and it's played at the River Club in Suwanee, Georgia. I live in a golf community, and I run into a lot of wealthy people right here in the neighborhood, so it made sense.

When I retired in 2008 Gina and I decided we'd start playing golf to do something different. I took a few lessons, and then I started playing golf with her. I was terrible! I'd never played golf before, but I picked it up quickly.

A month or two later, I started playing with other people. I was embarrassing myself, but I guess all new golfers go through that. I felt like I missed out on a lot by not playing golf before. I really love it, but I'm not addicted to it. I'm not a guy who's on the course every day.

Sometimes I feel bad being away from the house that long. I feel guilty. I play at least once a week, and if I don't have anything else to do, I might practice for an hour at the driving range.

A lot of people invite me to their tournaments, so I try to go and help them with my presence.

I do like golf, and I like riding motorcycles, and I also like flying my remote-controlled airplanes.

Motorcycle riding is a hobby I picked up my last year in Baltimore. I always wanted a Harley. I didn't ride when I was with the Braves because I tried to take care of myself, and I know the risks of riding.

But after my last year with the Orioles, I said, "Fifteen years in the big leagues. I think I deserve my first Harley."

I always wanted one. Gina's dad rode Harleys for 40 years. I bought one, and Gina got one too. She actually took me to my first motorcycle-riding lesson. I used to ride dirt bikes when I was a kid, so I had a little bit of experience. She wanted to learn how to ride too, so we both took lessons.

The Harleys were too much bike for a first bike. We took two or three lessons. When I jumped on my bike, I was pretty intimidated by it, especially the sound. So I started out only riding around the neighborhood.

When I saw Gina, I was more nervous about her being on the bike than I was about me riding it. I was really afraid because her bike weighed a lot and sat higher than mine. When that thing started, it was really loud.

She started riding around the neighborhood too. On the second lap, she couldn't control it and dropped the bike. Her heart was beating so hard. She walked straight home and was about to cry. She wasn't hurt, but she left the bike there. That was the end of that Harley.

I wound up selling her bike and bought her a Honda. She took a few test rides, but the memory of the day she fell was always in the back of her head. She held on to that fear, so she decided not to ride anymore.

I shipped that bike to Puerto Rico and gave it to my dad. He used it for a while and then sold it and got a bigger one.

Then I decided to buy a chopper. When I was doing that, Gina decided to give it one more chance. So we bought a trike. But the trike she wanted was a chopper trike. Again, it was too big and loud.

She tried it, but it was heavy and hard to turn. She felt intimidated. It only had 111 miles, and we sold it. It took three bikes for her to decide not to ride anymore!

By riding, I ended up meeting new friends. The people in the subdivision where I used to live have their own club. When I bought my Harley, I enjoyed riding with them. I also met a guy who has a chopper, and that's when I decided to get a chopper. Then I met more people in the hobby and joined a chopper club too. It's fun. My first Harley was a Fat Boy. I customized pretty much the whole bike. I looked at the different Harley paint sets, and I liked the one with the skull.

For some reason, I've always been fascinated with skulls. Not the mean-looking, devilish skulls, but more the funny, happy skulls. I put the skull graphic tank and fenders on the Fat Boy, and I changed all the aluminum to chrome. I like chrome.

I didn't like the wheels either, because they were solid with no holes. My father-in-law said they could be dangerous because the wind could move the bike more than normal. I put custom wheels on it, and I did the same thing for Gina's.

After that, I got the feeling that the bike was a little small for me. But it was too late because I had already customized it! After riding it for an hour, I felt uncomfortable. I wanted to be able to extend my legs.

Then I saw a Geico motorcycle commercial with a beautiful yellow Harley. I read that the Road Kings are bigger. I called Bruce Rossmeyer in Daytona, who was doing the commercial, the next day. I asked if they still had that yellow bike. He said they had just put it on the floor.

I asked what kind it was, and he said it was a customized Road King by Rocker Performance. I already had the Rocker Performance chopper. I was thinking of selling my Fat Boy and buying that one, but I didn't want to wait. I bought it right away.

I started riding the Road King. It was an awesome feeling. The seat was still kind of close, so I changed the seat. The one they made for me lets me stretch out farther. I can switch from long to short, depending on how I feel. It's a much more comfortable ride.

I was going to sell the Fat Boy, but because my dad and Gina's dad come to visit often, I decided to keep it. When they come, they can use the Fat Boy, and I can use the Road King. I kept it for a couple of years until I decided to start the baseball bat business.

Then I sold my two Harleys and put that money into my business. But it hasn't paid off yet!

I decided to keep the chopper. Who knows for how long? Now that we have Brody, Gina doesn't like to see me out riding on a motorcycle. She's afraid something might happen, and I don't blame her for that. I said I'd stop riding for a year or two.

I'm 40 years old. I could sell the bike, but then by the time I'm 50, I'll want to buy another one. So why not keep this one?

I rode with Andruw Jones once. He's got a really pretty Fat Boy, and I've ridden with Kevin Millar. He's got his own bike.

I wanted to sell or trade in this one, because now I want a custom cruiser. It's easier to ride through the mountains. The chopper is hard to ride through the mountains. It's so long that it's a challenge to go through the curves.

I don't ride by myself. There's always danger when you ride, but there's a lot more when you're by yourself because the cars don't respect you as much as when you're in a group of motorcycles. So most of the time I ride in a group.

Riding is just so much fun. It's a good feeling, going through the wind. It's a feeling only a motorcyclist can describe, especially if it's pretty outside. It's so scenic.

As a former catcher, I'm lucky my knees are good now. I've had surgery on both knees—a torn meniscus on the left (after the 1997 season) and the ACL on the right (1999).

My airplane hobby started before golf and before motorcycles. When I got called up to the big leagues in 1992 and came home from that season, I told Analy how all the players played golf or had some sort of hobby. I wanted to have a hobby.

Because some of my friends in Puerto Rico flew remote-control airplanes, I decided to talk to a guy in Ponce who sold them. I knew my friends flew airplanes, but I hadn't looked at them before.

I thought they were pretty cool, so I bought a trainer from Sam "Freddy" Bolien. I met him at the area where they fly, and he taught me how to fly it. After that first try, I didn't think I would pick it up because it's very hard. I was afraid to crash it, because a plane cost $300 or $400. But in order to learn, you have to crash a few!

Once I flew by myself for a good five minutes, I started to pick it up and was gaining confidence. The following day, I went out there and got better. Then I was taking off by myself. I crashed once taking off, but then he told me to accelerate when I took off and go as high as I could as fast as I could.

When I finally started flying by myself, right away I started looking at the magazines for my next plane. At one point, I had 20 airplanes. There was a time when the UPS truck was coming to the house every other day with accessories, parts, new engines, new airplanes, new this, new that!

Now I've got about 12 airplanes. I've had more than 50 come and go. I used to belong to GMA (Georgia Model Aviation), a huge area north of Atlanta where you can fly airplanes. There's lots of land.

By 2004 I wasn't flying as much, because I started a new life with Gina. But I kept all my planes, because I knew that sooner or later the fever would come back again. I'd have all my airplanes, even if they were out of date. I want to keep it simple, though, because today's planes are more complicated and sophisticated.

I DO MISS BASEBALL. I would think every player misses it when he retires—even if he doesn't admit it. It's a long, trying season with very little time off and not enough time with family. But it's such a rewarding profession, and the daily interaction and camaraderie with teammates is something special that I don't think you can get anywhere else.

Maybe someday I'll be back in baseball again, maybe as a coach. I would like that. But until then, I have a wonderful family and a wonderful life with a lot of good things going on every day to keep me busy.

APPENDIX

Javy Lopez on Atlanta Braves Career Leaderboard

Grand Slams	T-1st	7
Hits	5th	1,148
Total Bases	5th	2,008
Runs Batted In	5th	694
Extra-Base Hits	5th	418
Home Runs	6th	214
Slugging Pct.	6th	.502
At-Bats	6th	4,003
Batting Average	7th	.287
Doubles	7th	190
Games	8th	1,156
Runs	9th	508

Javy Lopez on Atlanta Braves Single-Season Leaderboard

Two-Homer Games	T-1st	8 (2003)
Homers at Home	T-3rd	26 (2003)

Javy Lopez's Career Batting Stats

YEAR	TEAM	AVG	G	AB	R	H	2B	3B	HR	RBI	BB	SO	OBP	SLG	OPS	AB/HR
1988	Gulf Coast	.191	31	94	8	18	4	0	1	9	3	19	.214	.266	.480	94.0
1989	Pulaski	.261	51	153	27	40	8	1	3	27	5	35	.284	.386	.670	51.0
1990	Burlington	.265	116	422	48	112	17	3	11	55	14	84	.297	.398	.695	38.3
1991	Durham	.245	113	384	43	94	14	2	11	51	25	88	.294	.378	.672	34.9
1992	Greenville	.321	115	442	63	142	28	3	16	60	24	47	.362	.507	.869	27.6
1992	Atlanta	.375	9	16	3	6	2	0	0	2	0	1	.375	.500	.875	—
1993	Richmond	.305	100	380	56	116	23	2	17	74	12	53	.334	.511	.845	22.3
1993	Atlanta	.375	8	16	1	6	1	1	1	2	0	2	.412	.750	1.162	16.0
1994	Atlanta	.245	80	277	27	68	9	0	13	35	17	61	.299	.419	.718	21.3
1995	Atlanta	.315	100	333	37	105	11	4	14	51	14	57	.344	.498	.842	23.8
1996	Atlanta	.282	138	489	56	138	19	1	23	69	28	84	.322	.466	.788	21.3
1997	Atlanta	.295	123	414	52	122	28	1	23	68	40	82	.361	.534	.895	18.0
1998	Atlanta	.284	133	489	73	139	21	1	34	106	30	85	.328	.540	.868	14.4
1999	Atlanta	.317	65	246	34	78	18	1	11	45	20	41	.375	.533	.908	22.4
2000	Atlanta	.287	134	481	60	138	21	1	24	89	35	80	.337	.484	.822	20.0
2001	Atlanta	.267	128	438	45	117	16	1	17	66	28	82	.322	.425	.747	25.8
2002	Atlanta	.233	109	347	31	81	15	0	11	52	26	63	.299	.372	.670	31.5
2003	Atlanta	.328	129	457	89	150	29	3	43	109	33	90	.378	.687	1.065	10.6
2004	Baltimore	.316	150	579	83	183	33	3	23	86	47	97	.370	.503	.872	25.2
2005	Baltimore	.278	103	395	47	110	24	1	15	49	19	68	.322	.458	.780	26.3
2006	Baltimore	.265	76	279	30	74	15	1	8	31	18	60	.314	.412	.727	34.9
2006	Boston	.190	18	63	6	12	5	0	0	4	2	16	.215	.270	.485	—
2006	Season	.251	94	342	36	86	20	0	8	35	20	76	.297	.386	.683	42.8
Minor Totals		.279	532	1,897	247	530	96	11	60	280	84	330	.315	.436	.751	31.6
Major Totals		.287	1,503	5,319	674	1,527	267	19	260	864	357	969	.337	.491	.828	20.5

Source: Stats LLC and TheBaseballCube.com

Javy Lopez's Playoff Batting Stats

YEAR	TEAM	AVG	G	AB	R	H	2B	3B	HR	RBI	BB	SO	OBP	SLG	OPS	AB/HR
1992	Atlanta/LCS	.000	1	1	0	0	0	0	0	0	0	0	.000	.000	.000	—
1995	Atlanta/Div	.444	3	9	0	4	0	0	0	3	0	3	.444	.444	.888	—
	Atlanta/LCS	.357	3	14	2	5	1	0	1	3	0	1	.357	.643	1.000	14.0
	Atlanta/WS	.176	6	17	1	3	2	0	1	3	1	1	.222	.471	.693	17.0
1996	Atlanta/Div	.286	2	7	1	2	0	0	1	1	1	0	.375	.714	1.089	7.0
	Atlanta/LCS	.542	7	24	8	13	5	0	2	6	3	1	.593	1.000	1.593	12.0
	Atlanta/WS	.190	6	21	3	4	0	0	0	1	3	4	.292	.190	.482	—
1997	Atlanta/Div	.286	2	7	3	2	2	0	0	1	2	1	.444	.571	1.015	16.0
	Atlanta/LCS	.059	5	17	0	1	1	0	0	2	1	7	.111	.118	.229	—
1998	Atlanta/Div	.286	2	7	1	2	0	0	1	1	1	1	.375	.714	1.089	7.0
	Atlanta/LCS	.300	6	20	2	6	0	0	1	1	0	7	.300	.450	.750	20.0
2000	Atlanta/Div	.091	3	11	0	1	0	0	0	0	0	1	.091	.091	.182	—
2001	Atlanta/LCS	.143	5	14	1	2	0	0	0	2	1	4	.200	.357	.557	14.0
2002	Atlanta/Div	.333	4	15	4	5	1	0	2	4	1	3	.375	.800	1.175	7.5
2003	Atlanta/Div	.333	5	21	1	7	2	0	0	0	0	6	.333	.429	.762	—
Totals		.278	60	205	27	57	14	0	10	28	14	40	.324	.493	.817	20.5

Source: Stats LLC and TheBaseballCube.com

Atlanta Braves' Yearly Finishes 1992–2003

Year	Pos.	Won	Lost	Pct.	GA/GB	Postseason
1992	1W	98	64	.605	+8	Lost WS
1993	1W	104	58	.642	+1	Lost LCS
1994	2E@Strike	68	46	.596	-6	No Playoffs
1995	1E	90	54	.625	+21	Won WS
1996	1E	96	66	.593	+8	Lost WS
1997	1E	101	61	.623	+9	Lost LCS
1998	1E	106	56	.654	+18	Lost LCS
1999	1E	103	59	.636	+6 ½	Lost WS
2000	1E	95	67	.586	+1	Lost Div
2001	1E	88	74	.543	+2	Lost LCS
2002	1E	101	59	.631	+19	Lost Div
2003	1E	101	61	.623	+10	Lost Div

MLB Record: Most Home Runs by a Catcher

Javy Lopez, 42 in 2003

Home Run	Date	Opponent	Pitcher
1	April 12	@Florida	Pavano
2	April 17	@Montreal (San Juan)	Ayala
3	April 17	@Montreal (San Juan)	Biddle
4	April 27	Milwaukee	Rusch
5	May 10	San Francisco	Nathan
6	May 11	San Francisco	F. Rodriguez
7	May 12	@Los Angeles	Brohawn
8	May 16	@San Diego	Peavy
9	May 22	@Cincinnati	Dempster
10	May 22	@Cincinnati	Dempster
11	May 23	NY Mets	Trachsel
12	May 24	NY Mets	Glavine
13	May 28	Cincinnati	Austin
14	June 5	Texas	Fultz

Home Run	Date	Opponent	Pitcher
15	June 7	Pittsburgh	Torres
16	June 7	Pittsburgh	Boehringer
17	June 8	Pittsburgh	Fogg
18	June 8	Pittsburgh	Fogg
19	June 11	@Oakland	Lilly
20	June 21	Baltimore	R. Lopez
21	June 21	Baltimore	Roberts
22	June 24	Philadelphia	Millwood
23	June 24	Philadelphia	Millwood
24*	July 20	NY Mets	Stanton
25	July 21	Chicago Cubs	Estes
26	July 21	Chicago Cubs	Remlinger
27	July 24	Florida	Penny
28	July 25	@Montreal	Manon
29	July 28	@Montreal	Biddle
30	July 31	Houston	Miller
31	Aug. 8	@St. Louis	Yan
32	Aug. 14	San Diego	Peavy
33	Aug. 14	San Diego	Wright
34	Aug. 19	San Francisco	Williams
35	Aug. 31	@Pittsburgh	Lincoln
36	Sept. 3	@NY Mets	Moreno
37	Sept. 7	Pittsburgh	Wells
38	Sept. 9	Philadelphia	Wolf
39	Sept. 10	Philadelphia	Padilla
40	Sept. 13	@Florida	Willis
41	Sept. 17	@Montreal	Darensbourg
42	Sept. 20	Florida	Looper
43	Sept. 27	@Philadelphia	Telemaco

*Pinch-hit home run did not count toward overall record for catchers

Source: Retrosheet.org

Career Home Runs by a Catcher

Player	As Catcher	Overall
Mike Piazza	396	427
Carlton Fisk#	351	376
Johnny Bench#	327	389
Yogi Berra#	305	358
Ivan Rodriguez	304	311
Lance Parrish	299	324
Gary Carter#	298	324
Javy Lopez	243	260

Hall of Famer

Awards, Honors, Records, and Accomplishments
- Carolina League All-Star, 1991
- Southern League All-Star, 1992
- Southern League MVP, 1992
- International League and Triple A All-Star, 1993
- Caught Kent Mercker's No-Hitter (6–0 at Dodger Stadium), April 8, 1994
- Topps Rookie All-Star Team, 1994
- ESPY Baseball Play of the Year: 1995 World Series, Game 2
- Tied 2nd, Most Doubles in LCS (five in 1996)
- Tied 4th, Most Hits in LCS (13 in 1996)
- Tied 4th, Most Total Bases in LCS (24 in 1996)
- MVP, National League Championship Series, 1996
- Followed Keith Lockhart with last Braves back-to-back pinch-hit home runs, May 25, 1999, ninth inning, at Milwaukee
- National League All-Star, 1997, 1998, 2003
- NL Comeback Player of the Year, 2003
- NL All-Star Catcher (postseason), 2003
- NL Silver Slugger Catcher, 2003
- Braves Franchise Record, RBIs by a Catcher (109), 2003

Career Transactions

November 6, 1987: Signed by the Atlanta Braves as an amateur free agent

November 5, 2001: Granted free agency

December 7, 2001: Signed as a free agent with the Atlanta Braves

October 26, 2003: Granted free agency

January 6, 2004: Signed as a free agent with the Baltimore Orioles

August 4, 2006: Traded by the Baltimore Orioles to the Boston Red Sox for a player to be named (Adam Stern) and cash

September 8, 2006: Released by the Boston Red Sox

January 9, 2007: Signed as a free agent with the Colorado Rockies

March 12, 2007: Released by the Colorado Rockies

ACKNOWLEDGMENTS

I WANT TO START BY THANKING GARY CARUSO, WHO IS COMPLETELY responsible for making this book happen. He conceived the idea, convinced Triumph Books that my story was worth telling and would be well received by fans, and then did the hard work of turning his interviews with me into what you're reading. I don't think there are very many people who have more passion for baseball and the Braves than Gary does, and it was a lot of fun for us to be able to share our stories with each other.

Naturally, I want to thank my entire family, especially my wonderful wife, Gina, for their support throughout my life and my baseball career. Without them, there wouldn't have been much of a story to tell. I particularly want my dad, Jacinto Lopez, to know that my story also is his story. He's the one who drove my interest in baseball and was with me every step of the way, rarely ever missing a practice or a game when I was a youngster trying to become a ballplayer.

I owe a lot to the Atlanta Braves, because I spent most of my career with them. They gave me the opportunity to develop my talent, meet so many great people, and accomplish the things that I did. Few players in the history of baseball can match what I was a part of by being involved in 11 of the Braves' record 14 straight division titles.

I don't want to forget the fans! As I think you can tell by reading this book, the fans have always been extremely important to me. I want all of you to know how much I appreciated your interest and support of my career when I was playing and even today. Without the fans, there is no baseball on the professional level. I've tried never to lose sight of that. The fans don't get enough credit for driving baseball's popularity, but they've always been special to me.

During my career, I played in 1,503 games—and watched quite a few more, especially when Greg Maddux was pitching! No one can remember all the details from so many games, so I have to say that the websites Baseball-Reference.com and Retrosheet.org were particularly valuable in helping me remember and clarify many games and situations in my career. It amazed me how much information and statistics are available online, and thanks to Gary's iPad, we constantly were able to access the facts we needed within seconds.

And thanks to everyone at Triumph Books, of course, for believing in my story and bringing it to print.

—Javy Lopez

Working with Javy Lopez on this book was a fantastic experience, from beginning to end. Not only is Javy one of the greatest catchers in Braves history—and baseball history—but he also is an incredibly kind man who has remained humble and grounded throughout his success. In fact, it's impossible to imagine a ballplayer who could have been more receptive, cooperative, and gentlemanly than Javy throughout this project.

I wanted to do a book about Javy's life because I believed he had an interesting story to tell and also because I honestly think he was the Braves' most popular player in the 1990s. That's saying something, considering all the talent that passed through Atlanta-Fulton County Stadium and Turner Field in that remarkable era. If anyone deserved such immense popularity, it was Javy, because he couldn't have been more appreciative of the fans—then and right to this day.

Special thanks to my incomparable friends, Linda and Frank Catroppa, who opened their home to me and provided what they always do—positively unequalled hospitality (and nourishment)—while I was in Atlanta to interview Javy.

Thanks to everyone at Triumph Books, of course, for making this book possible. And, most of all, thanks to my wife, Lane, who never stops believing in me (as far as I know), and somehow puts up with my passions, especially for baseball and our Boston Terrier, Pumpkin.

—Gary Caruso